The Call from Within

Within

Accomplishing Your Meaningful Project

———————

Robin Wildt Hansen

For audiobooks, other books, newsletter, blog and
podcast, please visit:

www.robinwildthansen.com

It is a rough road that leads to the heights of greatness.

– Seneca

Contents

Introduction

Like everybody else, you have something unique to offer the world. It is what I call your Great Work. Deep down inside you may well know what it would be.

However, many of us reject the idea of our Great Work before we even get started.

This is usually because we believe that we wouldn't have the willpower to put it into practice. Or simply because we're afraid of the unknown.

This book will show you how to strengthen your willpower and increase your ability to stay conscious in situations that you are unaccustomed to. It will help you to consistently Take Action on that which makes your life meaningful.

You might not yet know what you have to offer the world. If so, this book will help put you on the right path. It will give you tools to make yourself Take Action on your current goals and incrementally raise your level of consciousness.

Perhaps you are one of the few people who know exactly what their Great Work is and are working on it right now. If so, I salute you. This book will help you make your process as effective as possible.

This is a practical guide that will help you identify the factors that aid you in your Great Work or your current goals as well as those factors that hold you back. It will help you enhance your strengths and overcome your inner resistance.

Throughout this book I will seek to influence you to internalise and consistently apply its ideas. If you do so, you will discover facets of yourself and of the world that are so awesome you probably would not have imagined they existed.

Part I

Success Factors

The fundamental pillars that keep your consciousness at a high level and support you in the accomplishment of your Great Work.

Chapter 1

Your Great Work

*"Every production of genius must be
the production of enthusiasm."*

– Benjamin Disraeli

What would your Great Work be?

Let me explain to you what I mean by that term. Your Great Work is the mission that will make your life meaningful.

Maybe at this moment in your life all you want to achieve is a larger income. That's fine. This book can help you get there, because it will give you tools for making yourself do your work in a consistent way.

However, money isn't really what I'm talking about in this chapter, and it isn't the full potential of what I am trying to help you accomplish in this book. I'm concerned with what will make your life meaningful.

We all have a certain calling that we feel will fulfil us.

Deep down inside, it is very likely that you already know what that calling is for you. In order to truly see it, you have to be ready to think big.

Your Great Work is your *individual* mission in the world. It isn't necessarily something that most people would agree is a noble, rational or profitable cause; but it is *your* Great Work.

Examples of Great Works

Here are some very different examples in no particular order, to give you an idea:

Einstein's Great Work of revolutionising Physics and our view of reality

Nelson Mandela's Great Work of getting rid of Apartheid in South Africa

Garibaldi's Great Work of uniting Italy

Casanova's Great Work of travelling and seducing women from all walks of life

Mother Teresa's Great Work for the poor in Calcutta

William Blake's Great Work of writing some of the most sublime poetry in the English language

Hernán Cortés' Great Work of conquering Mexico with an army of only 500 men

Alexander the Great's Work of conquering most of the known world.

The above examples seem out of reach to most of us. Most of us can't see ourselves accomplishing something at that level. However I selected these examples because they are famous and you have probably heard of them.

I can also provide you with some examples for the common person. They are from well-known movies and serials, so they are likely to be familiar:

High school chemistry teacher Walter White's Great Work of making enough money to put his kids through college after his impending death due to lung cancer (from Vince Gilligan's serial *Breaking Bad*)

Bookkeeper Guido's Great Work of helping his son survive the horrors of the concentration camp where they are both imprisoned by making him believe it is all a game (from Roberto Benigni's *Life is Beautiful*)

An unnamed corporate employee's Great Work of creating a way for himself and other men to emancipate themselves from the consumer society and reclaim their manhood (from David Fincher's movie *Fight Club* from the novel of the same name by Chuck Palahniuk).

Your Great Work is independent of judgement

As you can see, these Great Works are of varying moral value. They are not all judged as being morally worthy, or even profitable or rational from an outside perspective.

Furthermore, each Great Work probably seemed quite impossible and impractical to most people at the time the person started to Take Action on it.

That leads us to what they all have in common: The person dedicated his or her life to their Great Work, and was independent of other people's opinions about it.

This dedication is far more powerful than anyone's casual opinion or judgement.

Some Great Works can have bad results

A word of caution: Great Works succeed due to the passion and dedication of their author. Morality is not a requirement for success. This means that some unscrupulous people can accomplish their Great Work while doing harm.

This is not a reason to shun your own Great Work; on the contrary it is a reason why you must do your Great Work: as long as you are doing your Great Work, becoming fulfilled and living your own meaningful life, you gain gravitas. You are no longer as vulnerable to being sucked into the orbit of someone else's Great Work, and you are not the kind of person to take orders from an evil regime.

This is extremely important, not only because you then do no harm but perhaps even more crucially because as a human being, you are a node in a network: the things that you do or don't do, influence the people around you.

Your Great Work can change

Be aware that your Great Work isn't necessarily unchangeable all your life.

For instance, let's say that at this moment you are struggling with a debilitating disease that your doctor isn't helping you with as well as you would like. Your Great Work may then be to find a cure for yourself.

You make yourself independent of your doctor's and family's opinions and set out on your journey. Along the way you are forced to become conscious of the self-sabotaging parts of yourself that keep you from making a change that is radical enough to bring about the healing that you need so desperately.

Faced with the reality of your disease, you overcome your inner resistance and the resistance of other people every step of the way until you finally find true healing.

Now that you are healthy, your Great Work will take on a different form. At this point it may be to heal other people with the same disease that you had.

Or it may be something else. But the feeling of pursuing your new Great Work will essentially be the same: a feeling of deep satisfaction, of knowing that you are doing the right thing for you, and being happy with yourself while you are doing it.

Your Great Work is independent of circumstances

Think big when you identify your Great Work. Be open to every idea you have, no matter how crazy or irrational it may seem at first. Don't pay any attention to circumstances at this stage. Your Great Work doesn't obey circumstance; rather it is something that *changes* the circumstances of the world and of your life. So you must ignore circumstances when you identify your Great Work.

I'm not saying that you have to be an Einstein or a Mandela. For instance, my Great Work is to be a writer. That is not something that most people would think is particularly noble or world-changing. Most people would say that it isn't even likely to ever make me a living.

Other people can think what they choose about my Great Work, but I have no choice in the matter because my writing mission is in my Higher Nature.

Chapter 2

Your Higher Nature

*"For a man to conquer himself is the
first and noblest of all victories."*

– Plato

You can only achieve true individuality and happiness through your Higher Nature.

At first it takes effort to start living through your Higher Nature; but once you achieve it there is no limit to the happiness you gain access to. That happiness in turn motivates you to stay on the path of your Higher Nature.

I discovered this as I worked on the first draft of *The World*, my most demanding and transcendental novel to date.

I was writing in a cold, grimy and smelly studio apartment in central London. I would wake up every morning, freezing and breathing in the bad smell of the hot air vent; however I was happy because the night's dreams had given me fresh instructions for the day's writing.

Success Factors

One of my personal weaknesses is that when I'm tuned into my Lower Nature, I am extremely lazy. So if I had not been pursuing my Great Work I could easily have stayed in bed all day to avoid facing the cold. But since I was, my Higher Nature lifted me out of bed early every morning.

The first thing I did every day was to turn on my computer, then the kettle. When my tea was ready, so was my computer; I would sit down and instantly start writing, the tea and my typing keeping the cold at bay.

When I finished writing for the day, I would wander around London. I remember one day in particular. I was walking down Tottenham Court Road feeling the ecstasy of the creative force that was flowing through me. I had no idea how I would pull off such an ambitious work as *The World*, but I wasn't worried because I felt supported by my Higher Nature.

At one point, I happened to look at the people around me. I noticed that several of them looked stressed. It was so strange to me; at that moment I simply couldn't fathom why anyone would be stressed. Although I had been stressed many times before in my life, at that moment I was too far removed from it to even understand the concept.

The reason I am telling you all this is not because I want to brag or make you feel bad. On the contrary, my point is that this creative energy is available to anyone who chooses to access it. I want to motivate you to do just that and pursue your own Great Work.

In general, however, I don't talk about the creative ecstasy I feel or any other aspects of my own success or fulfilment.

There are two reasons for this:

1. It is far more important to Take Action than to talk about it;

2. Talking about what you plan to do can often prevent you from actually Taking Action, because when you talk about it you shift your energy away from accomplishing things and over to convincing other people of the rightness of what you want to accomplish.

For now, I hope I have managed to at least make you a little bit more motivated to become attuned to your Higher Nature and pursue your Great Work.

Chapter 3

Your Soul

"Destiny is usually just around the corner.
Like a thief, a hooker, or a lottery vendor:
its three most common personifications.
But what destiny does not do is home visits.
You have to go for it."

– Carlos Ruiz Zafón, *The Shadow of the Wind*

There was a man named David Barrier who was a good driver and very proud of that fact. He knew his way around his city like very few others, and he drove with confidence.

One day, David had a meeting scheduled at a company that was located on Abundance Avenue. This sounded like a large thoroughfare, so it seemed strange that he had never heard of it. The fact that he didn't know about it made him doubt that it existed.

It annoyed him that the company had established itself on a street he didn't know of. In fact, before driving off to the meeting he set aside a great deal of time to complain to his colleagues that any company would locate its headquarters on such a ridiculous-sounding street. When his colleagues asked him why he didn't look at a map or use his car's navigation system, he looked at them as if they were crazy.

"I know this city," he said with a menacing glare. No one dared or bothered to contradict him.

He set out in his car. He drove around the city looking for the unknown street. He had some ideas about where it might be.

He tried a few of his ideas. However after he had been to three different neighbourhoods, he still hadn't found the street. The time of the meeting was drawing near, and he started to worry that he might be late.

He called his office to double-check the address. They confirmed it. One of his colleagues started to explain how to get there. But David stopped him.

"I know this city," he repeated.

"Ok," his colleague said.

David had run out of ideas, so he decided to turn on his navigation system after all. This was a desperate measure because he hated the voice of the navigation system. It was a nagging voice, and he couldn't imagine that it could have anything to teach him.

However at least it wasn't as embarrassing as being educated by his colleague.

The navigation system located Abundance Avenue and started guiding him. However, at a crucial point he didn't hear it instructing him to turn because he was talking very loudly on the phone telling a friend about a big deal he had struck the previous week.

"I knew this navigation system was useless," he said to himself, discovering that he had missed his turn.

However, he had seen the place on the map of the navigation system. Knowing his city well, he found the place himself without taking another look.

"I'm sorry about being late," he said upon arriving at the meeting. "It was the stupid navigation system."

"It's all right," the people in the meeting room said and found him a chair.

A few months later David's boss sent him to a meeting in another city called "Los Angeles".

David didn't believe the city existed; he was of Spanish ancestry and he knew that the name meant "The Angels". He found it hard to imagine that any city in the real world could have such a ludicrous name. He had a sneaking suspicion that his boss was playing a practical joke on him.

He was motivated to go, however, because he had been told that if the meeting went well he would get a big promotion.

This time he complained to his colleagues for an entire week about the city whose name sounded like a fairy tale. Some of them tried to tell him that Los Angeles is a very well-known city, and some of them told him that they had even been there themselves.

He wouldn't listen. "Los Angeles! What will they think of next," he kept repeating.

He insisted so much that when he finally set off, although he was generally well-liked, his colleagues breathed a sigh of relief.

He drove to the edge of his city, but since Los Angeles was very far away, there was no sign pointing to it. He drove all the way round his own city on the ring road but still didn't see a sign.

"It is as I said," he thought. "Los Angeles only exists in my boss' head."

For a moment he considered turning on his car's navigation system just to make double sure that Los Angeles didn't exist.

But then he remembered how the stupid navigation system had made him lose his way the last time. He didn't want that to happen ever again.

So he turned his car around and drove back, convinced that Los Angeles was nothing but a dream. I hear that he believes it to this day, no matter how many people he meets who tell him that they have been there.

David's boss was not happy. He let him keep his job, because he was very good at what he did. However, he never promoted him again. David had reached his success limit.

Self-imposed limits

In this simile, the navigation system is the soul. Your soul knows the whole world and can guide you anywhere. It can take you to heights that you cannot possibly fathom until you have actually experienced them.

It will do so if only you don't impose limits on yourself.

The trouble is, we impose limits on ourselves most of the time. The purpose of this book is to teach you to overcome those limits in an incremental and sustainable way.

Your soul is the part of you that knows what lies beyond your current limits. It attracts you to what is as yet unknown to you.

If you feel a powerful calling towards something that doesn't quite make sense to you yet, then that could be the calling of your soul.

Genius

What I call the soul is enshrined in the ancient Roman concept of the "genius", which has given rise to the modern English word of the same name.

In ancient Rome, a genius was a personal guardian spirit that was worshipped in the private home of the individual.

The word is related to the Latin verb *genui*, "to create". So any individual who achieved great things or who was particularly creative was said to have a powerful genius.

Your soul is that part of you that spurs you on to be a "genius".

It makes you pursue your Great Work. Your Great Work, after all, is a work of genius.

The Myth of Talent

The Myth of Talent is very deeply ingrained in our culture. We tend to think that a person is either born a genius or will never become one.

However, that is an erroneous and unproductive idea.

Any human can carry out a work of genius. The key to being a "genius" is to trust your soul to lead you to places you didn't know existed. It's what Eckhart Tolle calls "the power of not knowing."

Tolle writes:

"If you can be absolutely comfortable with not knowing who you are, then what's left is who you are – the Being behind the human, a field of pure potentiality rather than something that is already defined. Give up defining yourself – to yourself and others. You won't die. You will come to life."

The point I am making here is that it's far more difficult than we think to get out of our own way and allow success to happen for us.

In his audio course, *Manifesting Your Destiny*, Wayne Dyer says:

"Your job in this whole business of manifesting is not to say how or when but just 'yes'."

Don't be like David Barrier who reached his limit because he wanted to micromanage the "how" and hold on to previous definitions of himself. David Barrier was so attached to his self-definition as a great driver and navigator that he insisted on deciding how he would reach his destination; if he couldn't reach his destination in the way that would protect his ego then he preferred not to reach it at all.

The point is, you can only get so far with your current definitions of yourself and reality.

Most people compromise and accept that they can only get so far. They go for the consolation prize of protecting their image.

However, if you want to go really far in life, if you want to accomplish your Great Work, then you have to let go of those ideas that won't take you to your destination.

Manifesting your deepest desires is about *allowing* your desires to manifest. Your soul is already working on manifesting; your job is to allow it to happen. That is why everyone who talks about manifesting says that you must formulate your intentions in phrases that are positive, universal and in the present tense: if you think and speak in that way, you do not block manifesting.

When you express yourself like that, you are speaking the language of the soul. What does that tell you about the soul?

Well, if you express yourself in a positive, universal and present way then it is impossible to complain about anyone or anything. It is impossible to ask for something that will be just for you and to specify that so-and-so shouldn't have it. And it is impossible to brood over the past or worry about the future.

This is because every soul is directly plugged in to the universal force that creates everything in the eternal now.

Some people call this force "the universe"; some call it "God" or the "Tao". I will not get involved in what you or anyone else chooses to call it.

The ocean and the glass

It has been said that if God (or whatever you choose to call it) is the ocean then your soul is a glass of that water. This means that the entire creative power of

Success Factors

God (or the Universe, or the universal creative force or whatever you choose to call it) is available to you.

That is why there is no limit to what you can manifest. It is also why you have to go through your soul to truly create something new.

Your soul doesn't care what people think of you, so it doesn't impose limits upon you.

Your ego is highly invested in your image, and will do all it can to broadcast your praiseworthy deeds and hide your embarrassing actions. This leads to basing your decisions on how they might look to others.

The soul, on the other hand, doesn't care how many people you have managed to convince that you are a good person. It knows exactly who you are.

The advantage of this is that you can gain a better relationship with your soul without having to worry about advertising your good deeds or covering up your mistakes. You can focus on your thoughts and actions with the quiet knowledge that you are being effective and moving in the right direction.

When you do this, you are not motivated by what other people think you should be doing. You tap into the motivation of your soul to accomplish your Great Work. It is what I call Deep Motivation.

Chapter 4

Deep Motivation

"To believe in something, and not to live it, is dishonest."

– Mahatma Gandhi

Countless books have been written about motivation and how to motivate yourself. However to my mind most of them don't approach this subject from the most useful perspective.

To me the most burning question is not *how* to become motivated but *why* it would be necessary to learn motivation in the first place.

After all, we're talking about the motivation to pursue your heart's desire.

It is what I call Deep Motivation: the motivation to carry out your Great Work.

Why would you need to motivate yourself to pursue *that*?

It's obvious why you would lack motivation to do something that you *don't* want to do – I mean that is the reason most people study self-development:

they're fed up with their routine, and they have a deep longing to do something meaningful.

I think it is the situation of 99% of people who buy self-development products. I used to be in that situation myself, and I read a lot of self-development literature in that period.

This is why self-development products are mostly geared towards taking that first step of getting out of your routine and starting something new of your own design.

It is indeed a key hurdle, because although at the time you have a lot of motivation to take that step, you need more than just motivation in order to make that leap of faith: you need to mobilise a critical mass of *courage*.

However this book is mostly about what to do after you've quit your day job: **after** you've burned your bridges.

This is the next key hurdle because after you've burned your bridges you are in very real danger of failure.

The problem is that people find it hard to tap into their Deep Motivation to do the thing they *most* want to do.

I know it sounds incredible, but think about it: If everyone were 100% motivated to fulfil their life's mission, most people would be happy.

They would be doing what makes them happiest, and they would be satisfied with their lives.

People wouldn't meddle in each other's lives. Happy people don't meddle in other people's lives because they're already fulfilled by their own life. They don't need to look anywhere else.

If people were living through their Higher Nature, they wouldn't have time for drama. They would be getting on with their Great Work of making the world a more beautiful place in their own unique way, and their Great Work would be giving them the satisfaction that we all need.

Crime and warfare would be significantly reduced. The planet we live on would be a far more well-functioning and harmonious place.

I'm not saying that everyone would love their neighbour; I'm simply saying that people wouldn't see the point in messing with their neighbour's life because their own life would be rich enough.

One of the reasons why there is so much drama and unhappiness in this world is that most people don't make that first leap of faith and burn their bridges.

Once you have burned your bridges and the only alternative to success is very public failure, then you have a lot of leverage with yourself; you have powerful reasons to be motivated because you have a lot to lose by not Taking Action.

And yet you are still in danger of not taking action that is *massive enough* to allow you to succeed at your Great Work.

This is the point when you start to realise how much effort is actually involved in accomplishing your Great Work.

You may have been able to motivate yourself moderately to take moderate action when you had a boss and deadlines breathing down your neck.

And you may have had very powerful motivation to get out of there.

But when it comes to actually doing your Great Work, you are your own boss, and the motivation has to come from you, not someone else.

Furthermore, moderate motivation and moderate action are not enough when it comes to your Great Work. You need to channel your Deep Motivation to massively Take Action.

Chapter 5

Taking Action

*"To be idle is a short road to death
and to be diligent is a way of life;
foolish people are idle, wise people are diligent."*

– The Buddha

Taking Action is the most crucial component of accomplishing your Great Work.

This is not only because you can't *accomplish* anything if you don't *do* anything but also because happiness comes from Taking Action.

You don't get happiness from the fruits of your labour but from your labour itself.

This can be a very hard concept to grasp because we have been so thoroughly trained to focus on results. Most of us have conditioned ourselves to only Take Action if we believe we have a good chance of reaping a reward that is more valuable than the effort we put in.

This is an approach that ultimately leads to unhappiness and chronic dissatisfaction.

If you invest your happiness in the *results* of your actions, then obviously your happiness will depend on the results that you get.

The consequence of this is that if the results don't fulfil your expectations, you will have no choice but to be unhappy with the action you took. You will blame yourself and everybody else for the *effort* you put in.

This is dangerous because it means that you start resenting your own effort.

The more resentment you invest in your actions, the more you will resent the effort you put in when it doesn't result in the exact outcome you are going for.

It is important to avoid resentment because it leads to a downward spiral where Taking Action becomes more and more cumbersome because of all the negative emotions you have associated with it.

If you enter this downward spiral then when you *do* manage to overcome your own resentment enough to Take Action, and you don't get the exact result you were going for, you will resent your efforts even more.

This can go on endlessly until you grind to a complete halt.

It is the syndrome of someone who says:

"I put in so much effort hoping to make 1,000 sales, but I only made 675. I'm a failure."

Or who says:

"I help other people so much, but no one appreciates it. No one does anything for me. People are thoughtless and ungrateful."

Both statements belong to a pattern of blame: blaming yourself or other people. It ultimately comes down to the same thing: unhappiness and resentment of the action that is necessary to succeed.

That kind of attitude will not allow you to take the massive action that is necessary to succeed at your Great Work.

You have to *love* Taking Action, or learn to love it.

As difficult as it may be to overcome your Lower Nature and get into the flow of almost effortless action, once you achieve it, Taking Action becomes sublime ecstasy.

So, how do you get to that point?

Chapter 6

Self-Discipline

"In war there is no prize for runner-up."

– Seneca

As mentioned in the previous chapter, if you want to succeed at your Great Work you have to get into the positive flow of reaping happiness from Taking Action. Your happiness has to be independent of the results you are getting.

Although it is an effortless flow once you are there, you have to *get* there first. Self-discipline is the way.

Self-discipline is the rocket fuel that will get you through the gravitational field of your Lower Nature.

Again, this might not sound like much fun.

But it is. It's incredibly exciting when you begin to see what you can accomplish if you pursue a long-term goal and have self-discipline on your side.

Again, we have been conditioned by our consumer society to shun self-discipline.

We have been taught not to make an effort and to believe that there are products out there that will solve any problem we may have.

Some examples:

- If you feel that life is meaningless because you don't have the courage to get on with your Great Work, you can pop a pill that will allow you to keep leading a life that goes against your own beliefs, without having a nervous breakdown or committing suicide.

- If you are unable to concentrate due to indulgence in junk food, passive social media consumption and drama, your smartphone will do the thinking for you.

The message is that it is all right to go through life without ever taking a stand or improving yourself. It is all right to slowly become softer, stupider and sicker. People who believe this message are easily reduced to passive, unconscious employees, consumers and patients.

However, if you want to wake up to your true individuality through your Great Work, you have to refuse to be a passive resource.

You are a human being and you have great power that you can use for your own unique purpose. But you can only use it at its full and lasting potential if you build up Self-discipline.

If you don't accumulate the discipline that is necessary to use your power for your own purposes, someone who is more disciplined will use your power for theirs.

Part II

Failure Factors

The holes in the road you need to watch out for because they can lower your level of consciousness, steal your time and prevent you from accomplishing your Great Work.

Chapter 7

Your Lower Nature

"You can never get enough of what you don't need."

– Eric Hoffer

Our consumer society relies on and encourages our Lower Nature. Your Lower Nature is focused on what you can *get* and what corners you can cut in order to do as little as possible. This is why people who live through their Lower Nature are greedy consumers, unquestioning employees and generous patients.

Your Lower Nature likes stimulation, be it through television, social media, junk food, drugs, new clothes or pornography.

It will willingly consume all these things as long as it doesn't have to *do* much for them.

Your Lower Nature is lazy. It wants to get as much as possible while expending the least possible effort.

At the first glance this may seem reasonable; after all, we have been trained to think in terms of investment and return.

Failure Factors

We have been trained to think that the less we have to do and the more we can get, the better.

So let's try to examine this idea and see if it works.

There are certain things that your Lower Nature gets a kick out of getting.

I won't talk about sex here, because sex is something you can practise through your Lower Nature or your Higher Nature, depending on how you do it and who you do it with.

So let's focus on consumer products, sugar, junk food, alcohol and drugs. These are all treats that appeal exclusively to the Lower Nature.

Let's say that today you have eaten a delicious cake, bought a new pair of jeans and enjoyed a great dinner with a glass of good wine. Let's say you feel pretty good.

Now let's say I were to fill 20 trucks up for you with sugar, new designer clothes, drugs, alcohol and junk food, and have it all delivered at your doorstep. Are you happy now? It is likely that you will experience momentary elation and perhaps post photos on your social media profile. But you won't experience deep happiness from having all this stuff delivered to you.

So let's take it one step further and see if we can find happiness there. Let's say you start consuming all this sugar, new designer clothes, drugs, alcohol and junk food. You're still not quite happy, so you keep going until you have consumed the entire twenty truckloads. Now have you found ultimate happiness?

You would never achieve happiness that way. You can't achieve happiness through your Lower Nature. You can achieve pleasure, but not happiness.

Pleasure is limited. As you eat, drink, dress and snort yourself through those truckloads of stimulation, your pleasure can only increase up to a certain point. After that, if you continue, your pleasure will gradually diminish and ultimately turn to disgust.

True happiness is unlimited and is actually the nature of the universe itself. But it is not accessible to the Lower Nature.

That is why the entity that lives through the Lower Nature dreams mostly of power, wealth and fame but never of happiness.

That entity is the ego.

Chapter 8

Your Ego

*"Many could forgo heavy meals, a full wardrobe,
a fine house, etcetera. It is the ego they cannot forgo."*

– Mahatma Gandhi

The neighbours

Once upon a time there were two neighbours who were always fighting. They would curse each other all day, and their curses were so loud and vile that they rose all the way to heaven and disturbed the peace of the angels and even of God himself.

One day, God decided that he had had enough. He summoned the souls of the two neighbours to come and see him in heaven. He told them that it was high time they guided their humans away from this ugly waste of their gifts and towards their Great Work.

"We've been trying to do that all their lives," the souls protested. "But to no avail."

"Make them understand the benefits of the right path," God said. "Show them they can manifest anything they want."

"But we've been demonstrating that to them all their lives!" the souls protested.

"It would seem," God said, "that they were unable to read your subtle signs. You have my permission to really spell it out for them. In fact, *say* it to them, word for word. Now go!"

The soul of the first neighbour descended, taking on the form of an angel with white wings and a halo bright as the sun.

The man was standing on his porch, binoculars in hand, looking at his neighbour's house as his soul approached. He was struck by supreme awe when he saw the angel descending. He threw himself to the ground.

"Have mercy on a wretched sinner," he begged. "Starting from today I promise to mend my ways. Just don't make me roast in hellfire as I know I deserve."

"Do not be afraid," his soul said. "I have not come to punish you but to fulfil your greatest wish."

"My – my greatest wish?" the man asked.

"Yes."

"Does it have to be a noble wish or can I ask for anything?" he said, thinking of the lottery ticket he had bought that day.

He didn't know it, but in fact his motivation *was* noble; he had bought the lottery ticket thinking that if he won the lottery he could help his daughter, who had just had a baby with a man who wasn't much of a provider. Furthermore, he could have his house repaired. He had recently discovered it was full of rot.

"You can ask for anything," his soul replied. "However there is one caveat: No matter what you ask for, you will get it. But your neighbour will receive twice as much of the same thing."

The man was aghast. He hated his neighbour too much to give him anything, even if he didn't lose anything by it. The thought of living in a house full of rot and not being able to help his daughter and grandson was extremely painful for him. But he simply could not bring himself to help his neighbour.

"Then I don't want anything," he said.

"Are you sure?" his soul asked, taken aback.

"Yes," the man said, looking down and shifting his feet in regret. "I'm sure."

Now the soul of the other neighbour descended, also in the form of an angel but on the other side of the fence. He made the same majestic appearance at the second neighbour's doorstep.

The same interaction ensued, up to the time when the soul asked the man what his wish was and stated the condition.

The man was dismayed, but he didn't refuse the offer outright. He thought about it for several minutes. Then he looked up, a sly expression on his face. He told his soul that he had decided on an intention that he wished to manifest.

"What is it?" the angel asked.

"I want to lose one testicle," the man said.

Success and failure barriers

This story is an example of how our ego can make us get in our own way. The reason it does this is that when we are ruled by our ego, we do not see reality.

If those neighbours saw reality, they would see how their heart's desire is available to them, and that even if their neighbour were also happy, that would not detract from their own happiness.

The reason they chose to stay miserable was that instead of seeing reality, they saw the stories they were telling themselves about how they had been wronged by each other.

Your ego is not anything in itself but rather a collection of ideas about what the events and facts of your life say about who you are.

The events and facts of your life, such as your age, appearance and accomplishments, have been undergoing constant change ever since you were born. Even your intellect and opinions have changed.

The logical conclusion is that you are not an unchangeable person who remains the same all his or her life.

No human being is the same all his or her life; both mentally and physically we keep changing.

But we hate that idea.

That is, our egos hate that idea.

Through all your changes, your ego has been scrambling to adapt to reality to seem like it really is the *true story* about you and always has been.

This means that it must camouflage the fact that it is a description that keeps changing.

Tricky business. It is very difficult for your ego to keep the story of you attuned to the changing facts of your life whilst insisting that your story must be consistent, in the sense of describing one single, unchanging identity.

So your ego doesn't want you to change too quickly.

This is one reason why you have success barriers: it would be too hard to instantly adapt the story of who you are to a radically different life situation. Even on a physical level, modification of identity is an exhausting process, because it requires rewiring of the brain. Your brain will resist rewiring itself to such a great extent until you prove you are ready for this new identity, this new ego.

But there are also failure barriers: someone who used to be someone will cling to their old self-image after they have lost their previous identity. We have all seen an old man go on and on about how "back in the day" people used to treat him with respect and even awe. To his young listeners, it sounds pathetic. To him, on the other hand, the past is the only place where his ego story still makes sense, so it is the only place he can tolerate.

The ego is heavily invested in image. The ego is a big part of the reason people choose to break their backs working for corporations, spending most of their life on activities that they personally find meaningless.

Often what motivates them is not what they do but the image they get from their career. They are dependent on the praise of their boss and the respect of the people whom they hope they are impressing with the status and income they have achieved.

It is paradoxical that when you start Taking Action on your Great Work, such people are likely to tell you that your pursuit of your dream is "egotistical".

The contrary is true, because the only way you can fully pursue your Great Work, that is the desire of your soul, is by disconnecting from your ego's dependence on image. This is the only way you can truly go your own way.

To do this you must become "independent of the good opinion of other people", as the psychologist Abraham Maslow put it.

This is the way to true self-esteem, because once you are in harmony with your soul and pursuing your Great Work, you are making yourself happy and have your own good reason for loving yourself.

Failure Factors

Your ego, on the other hand, can never give you true self-esteem.

This is because self-esteem is what you think of yourself, while ego is what you think other people think about you.

I don't know who first said this, but it is very true.

This is why the ego is such a source of pain: if you depend on the good opinion of others, you will continuously be chasing satisfaction because you cannot control everybody's opinion about you. If you try you will have to constantly modify your image to please others.

It is highly stressful and exhausting to constantly rewrite your personality to suit other people. Such activity won't leave you a whole lot of energy to pursue your Great Work. Furthermore, since you can be certain that you will never reach the point where everybody will approve of or understand your Great Work, you will never truly get started.

If you do try to start out while being dependent on the good opinion of others, you will probably get stuck in procrastination.

Chapter 9

The Light Side of Procrastination

"If it weren't for the last minute, nothing would get done."

– Rita Mae Brown

What are the obstacles to getting on with the work that you know is meaningful for you?

We commonly use the umbrella term "Procrastination" to cover any internal cause that keeps us from doing what we are supposed to be doing.

The classic image of procrastination is someone who is under the pressure of a deadline but who still spends time clearing up their home, checking their social media feed or reading articles on Wikipedia or news sources. Then the deadline comes dangerously close. They panic, and that is what saves them. The panic gives them the impetus to pull themselves together. There is a spurt of effort and the procrastinator somehow manages to submit his or her paper or whatever it is in the last few minutes before deadline.

Failure Factors

Many people romanticise this approach. I know I used to.

Once when I was at university I had an essay that was due at noon on a certain day. I started writing it at midnight the night before.

I got away with it: my essay passed and was given an OK mark.

It was a mess, though. I certainly didn't have the time or the mental stability to do a proper editing job in the wee hours of the morning as the deadline approached.

But if you want to accomplish your Great Work – something that you can truly call success on your own terms – then I guarantee you that the classic procrastination-followed-by-a-spurt-of-effort approach will not be sufficient.

However, that is still the light side of procrastination. Far more insidious is the dark side of procrastination.

Chapter 10

The Dark Side of Procrastination

"It works if you work it. You'll die if you don't."

– Alcoholics Anonymous

The scenario of starting to work just before the deadline is only the most recognisable face of procrastination. In fact it is only the tip of the iceberg.

As we know, it wasn't the 10% tip of the iceberg that sunk the Titanic but the 90% lurking below the surface of the water.

The tip of the iceberg isn't so bad: procrastination with a deadline usually ends with action being taken as the deadline approaches.

Far more sinister is the dark underbelly of the iceberg.

If you want a good life, a life with a direction determined by you that you can keep afloat whilst still staying generally on course, then you have got to keep a watch out for the varieties of procrastination where there is no official deadline.

I say no *official* deadline because even if no one tells you that you must get the job done by a certain date and time, there is always an *actual* deadline for everything in life.

One of the most extreme examples of an actual deadline is when you never got round to making a certain call, and in the meantime the family member or special person whom you meant to reach out to, passed away or permanently lost their memory.

An example that is more directly relevant to this book is the Great Work that you meant to start one day, and the realisation when lying on your deathbed that you have run out of time to do it.

Chapter 11

Stimulation

*"The human that depended on focused attention
for its survival now becomes the distracted
scanning animal, unable to think in depth,
yet unable to depend on instincts."*

– Robert Greene, *Mastery*

One of the most important obstacles to getting on with your Great Work is stimulation.

There are various categories of stimulation. Some of them work on the body first and through the body they affect the mind. Some work on the mind first and through the mind they affect the body.

What they have in common is that they tend to diminish your focus.

The kind of stimulation that enters your system through your body we may call *drugs*.

Drugs

The classical form of stimulation that we are warned against is drugs.

It is true that most drugs will diminish your focus.

What I am talking about here is anything that enters the system through the body.

This includes not only many illegal drugs but also alcohol, tranquilisers, antidepressants, sugar and junk food.

Most drugs appeal to the Lower Nature because they offer a high level of stimulation without demanding much effort in exchange.

Psychedelics can be a different matter if taken with great care and clear purpose. However, such practices go beyond the subject of this book.

On the whole, drugs can offer a quick fix and can sometimes help you accomplish things on the short term, especially when you are feeling sad, angry or otherwise indisposed to carrying out your tasks.

Or drugs can be used recreationally.

In both cases, when the drugs wear off and you need to get on with your work, it is usually harder to focus.

One solution can be to take more drugs. That can work on the short term, but it does mean that a period of recovery will be necessary at some point, which can take away from long-term progress at the other end. Furthermore, on the long term, taking drugs can result in health problems and a skewed view of reality.

By definition, if you want to accomplish something big then you have to be working on the long term. I'm talking years here. The best solution for that kind of timeframe is good health and clean focus.

"Information"

One of the greatest obstacles to clean focus is so-called "information".

This is an obstacle that is really worth focusing on because it is far less obvious than drugs.

We are often told that drugs are unhealthy. We are even (justifiably so) warned against junk food. However, "information" is usually seen as innocuous.

A key skill for accomplishing your Great Work is the ability to focus on a task for a sustained period of time.

Failure Factors

It seems obvious: if you want to accomplish something great, then what you can accomplish in one day will not be enough; you must be able to make a sustained effort for a long time.

However, this is a fact that is no longer taken for granted.

The reason that this fact is no longer obvious is that the world we live in today feeds us the illusion that we need to multi-task all the time.

The idea is that there is so much information on offer that we must change our focus as fast as possible in a constant race to avoid missing out.

In his book *Mastery*, Robert Greene writes that the ability to focus and learn from experience over a sustained period of time was what gave the human race an evolutionary edge over physically stronger animals.

Other animals live in the moment, and their capacity for learning from experience is severely limited. Consequently, they get weaker as they get older. Humans, on the other hand, have mastered a technique for making time work in our favour.

The way to learn mastery is to maintain sustained focus and gradually unravel the depth in whatever subject is your field of expertise. As you do so you are able to replace the strength and agility of youth with the deep understanding and experience of mastery.

Human beings have stereoscopic vision, which is designed for depth of focus. We have the most powerful brain on this planet, exquisitely developed for processing and using what we focus on.

The trouble is that these days we are being taught to replace that sustained focus with the quick fix of technology. It is as if we are trying to see the world through the eyes on the side of the head of the rabbit, which is constantly scanning its surroundings for threats.

We try to scan our way through the avalanche of information that overwhelms us every day in the form of emails, TV and social media notifications.

I'm sorry, did I say "information"? I don't really mean information, although this is what we call it for want of a better word.

The truth of the matter is that 99% of this "information" doesn't inform you at all.

So what is the nature of this "information" that prevents you from focusing? "Information" falls into certain categories:

Cute Entertainment

This is the amusing videos of fluffy animals or children that make you smile or laugh.

Social Media Wisdom

These are insightful quotations that are posted on social media.

Many such quotations are truly wise and are pithy formulations of the realisations that took great people entire lifetimes to arrive at.

The trouble is the context in which they are read.

These quotations are posted in bite-sized chunks and read by people who are extremely distracted.

Furthermore, the way in which they are served makes them look cheap.

When someone reads a bite of Social Media Wisdom, they usually feel a buzz.

However, they are only able to focus for long enough to feel that buzz and then click "Like" and/or "Share". As they click the button they are already in the process of forgetting what the quote was about.

This is a process that is harmful not only to the passive consumer but often even to the person posting the Social Media Wisdom. Why is this? Well, one common chain of events is the following:

Someone comes across a quote that immediately resonates deep in his or her soul. He feels the truth of the quote deep in his being. If social media did not exist he would probably examine it and think about what it means and how it relates to his own life.

However, at this point he remembers that he has a social media presence. So he posts the quote. Immediately, the emphasis shifts away from understanding and applying the quote to his own life. Now it is all about trying to look good in front of his social media followers. This is how true wisdom becomes an adornment of the ego and degenerates into Social Media Wisdom.

Pornography

Pornography appeals exclusively to the Lower Nature because it is stimulation that doesn't require Taking Action. That is why it is potentially harmful, just like any other type of "information".

It's the same mindset as with the other forms of "information": The consumer of pornography is overwhelmed by the unlimited abundance of stimulating videos available at the click of a button. He or she doesn't want to miss out.

Before the time of the internet, the porn user would treasure the exciting video that he would have gone through trouble and embarrassment to acquire. Now, however, he knows that he can reach the most stimulating part of this video and all the other videos on the internet at the click of a button.

This means that the entire porn process becomes one long string of climaxes.

Consequently, what happens in the brain of the modern porn user is that his dopamine receptors run wild. Dopamine – a neurotransmitter that is responsible for the brain's reward circuitry – floods the synapses. This is a similar process to the neurochemical response to snorting cocaine.

So the porn user fast forwards to the most stimulating part of each video in order to maximise his dopamine hit. Just like any other drug user, he needs to keep increasing the dose in order to numb himself from the realities of his life.

The long-term consequences are sad if the behaviour becomes addictive and compulsive: reality is greyed out and the porn abuser becomes more excited at the site of his laptop than by a sexy woman in real life. He needs more and more extreme porn at a faster and faster rate in order to keep his synaptic dopamine at the same level. In other words, he needs it just to feel normal.

The news

For the most part, even "the news" isn't information. It doesn't tell you anything that will help you improve your life. On the contrary it chiefly brings you stories that sadden and anger you and put you into a state of depressed apathy.

This is one of the most nefarious effects of the news: the feeling of powerlessness that it induces. When you watch the news, you are fed a narrative that says that the world is completely messed up and there is nothing you can do to change it.

It makes you feel that there is a vast gap between your life and the things that truly matter.

The implicit message is that you are living a meaningless life in a rotten world.

Think about *that* for a moment. Now *that* is a message of despair. It is the kind of message that makes people smoke dope and watch TV shows or surf conspiracy theories all day.

Failure Factors

Fortunately it is not only a message of despair. It is also a lie.

The truth is that you have a direct connection with the essence of life.

You have access to the unlimited source of power when you pursue your Great Work. You Great Work is the best thing you can do for the world. It is your unique way of making the world a happier and more beautiful place.

Chapter 12

"Information" and Unconsciousness

"An empty head is not really empty;
it is stuffed with rubbish. Hence the difficulty
of forcing anything into an empty head."

– Eric Hoffer

We have seen how exposure to "information" sabotages your efforts to accomplish your Great Work. But how do you avoid being exposed to it? After all, "information" is everywhere.

The first thing that is necessary in order to avoid being sabotaged by "information" is to really become conscious of how harmful it is. You need to build up supreme clarity about what this barrage of nonsense is capable of doing to your mind and to your life. That is the way to accumulate enough willpower to overcome it.

So let's take a look at the dark side of "information" and the consequences of indulging in it too much.

This is harder than it sounds because most people around you will constantly be telling you how common or even important "information" is, and how much a part of normal life.

As we will discuss in Chapter 14: "Other People", in the section on Mirror Neurons, human beings are constantly copying each other's thoughts, moods and behaviours. So you have to be conscious of what you want to achieve, and resist getting drawn in by attitudes or behaviours that hinder your success.

Such attitudes and behaviours are overwhelmingly abundant. In fact, they make up the general mood. It is most likely that the majority of the people you surround yourself with are caught up in such attitudes.

When people tell you to look at some "information", you must stick to your guns and remember all the hard work you have invested in building up your precious focus and positive state of mind.

Ultimately, it is up to you to determine how exposure to "information" will influence you at the time.

Maybe you have already done your day's work, and you still have some hours before bedtime. Maybe you estimate that this piece of "information" won't influence you so severely that it will reduce tomorrow's performance significantly.

Or maybe the temptation to watch "information" comes just as you are about to start working, when you have made your mind as pure as possible in order to do your best. Or maybe it comes just before sleeping, and you want to get the best possible rest in order to give your best the following day. In those cases you ight choose to resist the temptation.

When you walk the path of your Great Work you develop a highly sensitive radar for detecting factors that can degrade your state of consciousness.

Remember, you have a lot to lose. The people who are trying to influence you may not have anything to lose, because they aren't doing their Great Work. They aren't walking their own individual path. That is why they don't understand that you can't stop working for a moment to watch that item of celebrity gossip and send them a short, distracted message with a smiley to confirm that you watched it.

It can be very tempting to indulge yourself, both in order to please your acquaintances and because your Lower Nature knows that "information" gives you stimulation without requiring any effort in return.

However, as you progress on your journey you become more and more conscious of what such an indulgence would cost you in terms of focus and positivity. As mentioned, being aware of the true cost of "information" is something that really helps you stay away from it.

Another thing that helps is to focus on what you are doing, rather than on what other people are doing. This is because the way "information" keeps you from Taking Action is by distracting your attention from your own tasks and your own life.

"Information" feeds you the illusion that it is far more important to be informed about events taking place somewhere far off which ultimately you have no influence over.

The reality is that in order to Take Action you must focus on your own actions, not on anybody else's.

From a superficial perspective this may sound self-centred and egotistical. However while it may be self-centred, it is not egotistical. In fact, the only way you can make the transition from *talking* about making the world a better place to actually *doing* it is by giving your own unique gift.

You can only give your gift by focusing on it; not by throwing your arms up in the air in frustration over all the things that you can't do anything about anyway, or which it is not your mission to do something about.

This is an important point, by the way: there are many examples of people with good intentions who meddle in something they're not supposed to be meddling in. They tend to make things worse.

"Information" is stimulation

We have established that "information" generally isn't information because it doesn't really inform you. Its more prominent function is to allow you to feel emotions without actually doing anything to earn them; it allows you to stay within the comfort zone of your ego fantasies without entering into contact with reality, and still get the reward that would normally only come from Taking Action.

"Information" keeps you passive

The following are some of the ways that "information" keeps you passive:

Cute Entertainment gives you a warm and fuzzy feeling, and perhaps a spike of hard laughing. For a moment you get to feel like a bemused parent without having to do any of the work involved. In reality you are not making a difference in anybody's life; you are just watching some cheap entertainment.

Social Media Wisdom gives you the feeling that you are making changes in your life. It gives you the feeling that you are seeing deeper connections and processing things in a new way. In reality, however, you are not even leaving your office. You are still sitting there at your desk. Once you get over your "wisdom high" you will go back to making money for the corporation you work for.

Pornography gives you extreme dopamine spikes that in normal circumstances would be your endocrine system's reward to you for having improved yourself so much that you deserved to procreate with the sexy person on your screen. However in reality you haven't really changed except that now you are older.

The news makes you feel angry, sad and powerless. That really is the last nail in your coffin after the other types of "information" have made you feel that you have already accomplished everything there is to accomplish. The news tells you that you can't change anything. Is it any wonder that people these days feel confused about their direction in life? Is it any wonder that people never grow up?

"Information" has two functions:

1. To supply temporary relief from the pain of a purposeless existence and

2. To take you away from the focus you need in order to make your life purposeful.

What I am telling you is that if you want to accomplish something big, you must do the opposite of these two things. You must:

1. Face the reality of your life and whatever pain and pleasure this realisation may cause you and

2. Focus.

It doesn't sound very pleasant, does it? How much more pleasant would it be to be laughing at cat videos and indulging in daydreams about a glorious future that doesn't threaten your self-image because you know it will never come?

Far more pleasant.

The only trouble is that indulging yourself does not help you accomplish your Great Work.

Indulgence brings some pleasure, but ultimately it brings pain due to the time and opportunities lost along the way.

Opportunities may return, but time never does.

When that pain comes, the self-indulgent person feels he or she needs another hit of pleasure to cope with the pain. So he indulges in even more stimulation, which again brings pain so again he feels he needs another hit. It's a never-ending cycle of misery where the person gradually becomes softer and weaker and less able to Take Action to improve his or her life.

Indulging yourself will never bring you happiness. What it does is make you a greedy consumer, a generous patient and a mindless employee.

Unhappy people feed the economy

Unhappiness boosts consumption because it makes people reason through their Lower Nature and go for the consolation prize of stimulating products.

In order to buy the stimulating product, the unhappy person has to work hard to make other products that are sold to other unhappy people, and on and on. Then when junk food and depression has made the unhappy person ill, he has to buy medicine and treatments that are so expensive he has to mortgage his house to pay for them.

And yet I say that no one is really trying to control you, apart from your own ego. Someone may be taking advantage of your unhappiness. But you are the only one who can make yourself happy and free.

No one can control you if your ego isn't controlling you.

You have the option to do that which makes you happy. And if you do, then the entire cycle of misery will unravel and ultimately disintegrate.

People who are happy are people who don't have a hole in their self-esteem. So they don't need to buy a product to fill that hole.

Only unhappy people are addicted to stimulation.

This is the context in which "information" and other "agents" of unconsciousness should be seen.

The short-term effects

It probably won't make a big difference to your life if you watch that one animal/baby video before going to bed tonight.

Sure it may worsen the quality of your sleep because it stimulates you in a nervous and jittery way.

Sure it may cause you to operate at a lower level of consciousness tomorrow. This is because the influences you expose yourself to just before sleeping are crucial to your state of mind the next day.

However those effects are subtle, and you probably won't notice them on the short term, unless you're in the habit of attentively monitoring your own state.

The long-term effects

It is when we expand the timeframe that you see all too clearly what I mean. Over a decade or two the difference is vast.

It can be the difference between on the one hand accomplishing your Great Work, married to the partner of your dreams, living in a home that you are happy to come back to every day; and on the other hand trapped in a job you hate, married to someone you despise and living in a place you dread returning to at the end of the day.

Does it sound like I'm exaggerating?

I'm not. This is life or death. The changes you can make in your life if you follow the advice in this book are astronomical.

If you are still insisting that "information" isn't that bad, I would understand your objection; I know how innocuous "Information" can seem.

But it is exactly this appearance of harmlessness that allows "information" to creep up on you and infect your mind.

When you feel yourself succumbing to the temptation of "information", ask yourself what the long-term consequences will be for your life if you do this every day for the next decades.

Remember, your life is numbered in decades.

Focus

The point that I am making with you is that if you want to accomplish something big, then you must focus. In order to focus you must close the floodgates and shut out the millions of exabytes of nonsense that will otherwise wash over your consciousness like a tsunami over a candle flame.

Meditation vs. "information"

Meditation is one of the most effective practices that mankind has come up with for sharpening consciousness.

We will go deeper on the subject of meditation in the third and final part of this book.

Failure Factors

Most meditation practices are about focusing on a single object. That is they foster the exact opposite behaviour than "information" does.

In several of his discourses, the Buddhist monk and meditation teacher Ajahn Brahm tells the story of the time when he walked up the hill to his monastery.

In those days his presence was required in many places, so he had been driven up and down the hill for ten years without ever having walked.

However, on one particular day he had plenty of time and the weather was perfect. He told his driver to drop him off at the foot of the hill and he began to walk up.

The strangest thing happened: Ajahn Brahm could not recognise the hill. It seemed like a completely different place.

As he walked up, the colours of the vegetation seemed far richer than he was used to. He saw so many new things and discovered beauty he hadn't realised was there. Then he stopped walking. The colours became even richer and more details appeared.

On the surface it seems banal; obviously you notice more details when you are walking than when you are looking out of the window of a speeding car.

However it really seemed like a completely different place. It wasn't just that he saw more details of the same place; it was more like he was seeing a deeper and richer landscape than he was used to seeing from the car.

Ajahn Brahm thought of a scientific explanation: when you are whizzing past objects, the light entering your eye doesn't have time to translate into chemical images on the retina before light from new objects starts entering the eye and new superficial images are formed.

You could say that he was seeing the depth of the place whereas for the past ten years he had only been seeing its surface.

It is only when you slow down that you get a chance to see the depth in things.

I'm not saying that you should be a monk or lead a slow, withdrawn life. On the contrary, I'm advocating an active life where you do as many as possible of the things that you want to do. However, that is not the same as having an overstimulated mind that never gets to see the depth in things.

Failure Factors

An overstimulated mind doesn't get very far. It is like a dog chasing its own tale or a headless chicken running around the courtyard.

When you see the depth in things you are able to set a conscious course and make consistent progression.

This means that the road to higher consciousness and accomplishment goes in the exact opposite direction of multi-tasking.

If you want to accomplish something big, if you want to accomplish your Great Work, then you have to let go of any addiction to "information" that you may suffer from, and come back to reality.

A war to the death

I know that this seems like a very difficult thing to do. After all, "information" is everywhere.

However as mentioned, doing your Great Work is a war to the death.

It can be helpful to tune into that feeling of death. "Information" can kill you, not by shortening your life but by accelerating time so that it whizzes past you until you have no time left. Before you know it, ten, twenty, thirty years have passed. You lie on your deathbed with the realisation that you didn't do the things you had been sure that you would do "one day".

You didn't accomplish your Great Work. You didn't even connect properly with your loved ones. You spent minutes looking at nonsense on the internet. Those minutes added up to hours. The hours added up to days. The days added up to years. Years evaporated from your life.

On your deathbed you won't remember the "information" you have been looking at over the course of your life because in the greater scheme of things it isn't memorable at all.

Furthermore, "information" when consumed in excess has the effect of disconnecting you from reality, lowering your intelligence and causing mood swings.

Lowered consciousness

The abundance of "information" that has become available over the last couple of decades has given rise to an epidemic of lowered consciousness.

The movie *The Matrix* (1999) was almost prophetic on this subject.

Failure Factors

In the movie, each human being is housed in a "pod" and used to harvest bioelectric and biothermal energy to feed the machines that have taken over the world. The humans never move or do anything. They are essentially organic batteries.

The reason the humans are complacent about their situation is that they are unconscious of it. Thanks to a virtual reality matrix that keeps their minds stimulated, they think the human world still exists and that they are leading normal lives.

The events of their virtual lives keep their minds occupied and stimulated so they are too complacent to make the effort that would be necessary for them to wake up to consciousness.

The situation described in the movie is very much like many people's actual situation: a massive hamster wheel of working in a job they don't like to buy products they don't want while being kept unconscious through entertainment, social media, junk food, drugs, porn and unfulfilling sex.

We usually think of a human being as someone with his or her own thoughts, choices and opinions. However, such things are the prerogative of the few who have gone through the process of finding their true individuality.

This is because independent thoughts, choices and opinions demand effort.

It is difficult to muster that effort when you have so much stimulation available to you that requires no effort at all. That is why most people resist waking up and heeding the call of their Deep Motivation. They prefer the passive existence as human resources who are entertained and used for the purposes of others.

They have become matrix crops.

Matrix crops

The following is a list of symptoms of being a matrix crop, in no particular order. Matrix crops are:

- Unable to watch an entire movie without picking up their smartphone to check messages or scroll through their social media feed.

- Unable to focus on anything for more than a few seconds before their attention gets distracted.

- Compelled in conversations to start talking about something completely unrelated out of the blue.

- On a constant emotional rollercoaster no matter how stable their real-life context may be; you can see them one moment upset over some tragic story that popped up on their smartphone, demanding that you commiserate, and the next moment laughing hysterically over a video of an animal or child prodigy, having completely forgotten the tragic news that affected them so strongly only moments earlier.

- Suffering from chronic low-quality sleep because the last thing they do before sleeping is to indulge in "information", which puts them in an excitable emotional state.

- Envious of other people. Are convinced that other people's social media avatars should be taken at face value, and that they themselves are the only person in the world who has a normal job and is living a life of drudgery.

- Unable to focus enough to read a normal-length book.

- Unable to make a decision and then stick to it or, in some cases, even remember what it was.

Before the rise of the Internet, these traits described a socially disadvantaged segment of the population.

Now they describe most of us.

Chapter 13

Unconsciousness

*"We can easily forgive a child who is afraid of the dark;
the real tragedy of life is when men are afraid of the light."*

– Plato

Although recent years have seen a massive decline in the ability to focus, it is not that we were functioning at full brain power before the rise of the Internet.

The tendency to unconsciousness lies deep within human nature. Philosophers have been aware of this fact for millennia.

Indeed the ideas presented in *The Matrix* predate the movie by several thousand years.

They are found in one of the most influential myths of our culture, namely the Allegory of the Cave.

The Allegory is from Plato's book, *The Republic*, which was written approximately 2,400 years ago and is hugely influential to this day.

The Allegory describes a cave where people have been imprisoned from childhood. The prisoners are chained so that their legs and necks are fixed, forcing them to gaze at the wall in front of them and not look around at the cave, each other, or themselves.

Behind the prisoners is a fire, and between them and the fire is a raised walkway with a low wall, behind which people walk carrying objects or puppets that are depictions of real things.

The people walk behind the wall so their bodies do not cast shadows for the prisoners to see, but the objects they carry do. The prisoners can't see any of these things behind them and are only able to see the shadows cast upon the cave wall in front of them.

The sounds of the people talking behind them echo off the shadowed wall, and the prisoners falsely believe that these sounds come from the shadows.

To the prisoners, the shadows and echoes *are* reality, because they have never seen or heard anything else.

This is the situation that will also be described in Chapter 20, in the third and final part of this book in the section about the Two Minds in Buddhism: when the Doing Mind has completely taken over, all you see is the labels of the Doing Mind, and so you believe that the labels are reality.

Plato's Cave and The Matrix are both about the nature of reality. But what they depict is true for motivation too.

In the context of motivation, the light shining from the fire is your Deep Motivation while the shadows represent a weak reflection.

The shadows are shaped by others than you, so the weak reflection that you are seeing is not your own core Deep Motivation but the motives of others. Since you have never seen anything else, you will believe that the shadows are your own motivation.

That is why most people do feel a certain level of motivation to serve the shadows: the motives of other people for which they usually receive a pay check.

There is nothing wrong with working for a pay check or being motivated to do so. My point here is that if you want to accomplish your Great Work, you also need to access your Deep Motivation.

That is harder to do.

The prisoners are motivated, but their motivation is dull: it isn't shining with the light of inspiration.

At a certain point you may have felt a longing for that light that was so strong that you were compelled to commence a process of soul-searching in order to find a new path in life. Perhaps you are there now.

However there are many pitfalls on the way to the light. In *The Republic*, Plato poses the question: what would happen if one prisoner were freed and forced to turn and see the fire?

The light would hurt his eyes and make it hard for him to see the objects that are casting the shadows. If he were told that only now he is seeing reality, and that what he saw before was an illusion, he wouldn't believe it. In his pain, the freed prisoner would turn away and run back to what he can see without any pain or extra effort: the shadows of the objects.

We might say that he is running back to "information" and working for people who are more conscious than him.

This is why if you are Taking Action and your friend is not, your "prisoner" friend will often oppose your success, because your success is a beacon that reminds his true self that there is a world outside the shadows on the wall. His true self begins to awaken and quietly asks him to turn him towards the light.

The first encounter with the light is frightening for most people.

Plato writes, "...it would hurt his eyes, and he would escape by turning away to the things which he was able to look at, and these he would believe to be clearer than what was being shown to him."

This quotation inspired the following famous dialogue in *The Matrix*:

Neo: Why do my eyes hurt?

Morpheus: You've never used them before.

According to Plato, if someone were to drag the freed prisoner all the way out of the cave and into the sunlight, the prisoner would be angry and in pain, and his condition would only grow worse when the radiant light of the sun overwhelmed his eyes and blinded him.

Slowly, however, his eyes would adjust to the light of the sun. First he would only see shadows. Gradually he would see the reflections of people and things in water and then later the people and things themselves. Eventually he would be able to look at the stars and moon at night until finally he could look directly at the sun. Only then would he be "able to reason about it" and what it is.

The freed prisoner would now feel that the real world was superior to the world he experienced in the cave; he would be thankful for his liberation and would want to bring his fellow prisoners out of the cave and into the sunlight. So he would return to the cave with his new-found knowledge.

However, now that his eyes would be acclimated to the light of the sun, he would be blind when he re-entered the cave, just as he was when he was first exposed to the sun.

The prisoners would therefore assume that the journey to the real world had harmed him and that they are better off tied up in the cave (plugged into the "Matrix", as it were). Thus the returning prisoner would not receive the hero's welcome he had expected. In fact, the remaining prisoners might even kill him if he attempted to drag them out against their will.

So if you have learned to channel your Deep Motivation, to Take Action and get on with your Great Work, then expect resistance from friends, family and colleagues if you tell them or show them that you are Taking Action.

In the terminology of the Allegory of the Cave, the fact that you are overcoming your Lower Nature and actually Taking Action makes your "prisoner" friends, colleagues and family members feel that you are dragging them out into the light against their will.

Chapter 14

Other People

"Be independent of the good opinion of other people."

– Abraham Maslow

Once you start overcoming your own Lower Nature, you will come up against the Lower Nature of other people.

You really start noticing it in other people when you accomplish something that is generally seen as impressive.

If you tell someone about it, you will at first expect them to be impressed and happy for you.

Maybe this is indeed their attitude. If so, you have a very good friend, colleague or family member and you can be pretty sure that this is a person who to some extent is overcoming his or her own Lower Nature.

However in most cases their first unconscious response will be to think, "What does this say about *me*?" This is often true even for someone who is close to you.

The reason is that their ego is always writing and rewriting the story about their identity and scanning their environment for information that they judge in a way that makes their personal story seem plausible and justified.

They will then react to you based on what they feel about themselves.

Why is this a failure factor for you? After all, it's other people and not you, right?

Mirror neurons

Research conducted primarily on monkeys but also on humans has demonstrated the existence of so-called "mirror neurons".

Mirror neurons are neurons that fire both when the individual is performing an action and when he, she or it is observing the same action performed by another.

In other words, to those neurons there is absolutely no difference between you performing a certain action and seeing someone else doing it.

What are the wider implications of mirror neurons regarding the way we relate to other people?

It doesn't take much imagination to conclude that our minds are not isolated from one another.

Other people's minds are like a network that your mind is plugged into. The influence that other people's minds exert on yours is proportional to how close you are to them.

This gives fresh validity to motivational speaker Jim Rohn's saying that "you're the average of the five people you spend the most time with."

Jim Rohn's words mean that although we tend to think that our thoughts and emotions are our own, we are really soaking them up from the people around us.

So you must choose your influences very carefully in order to keep your mind in a focused and energised state for taking positive action.

Other people's procrastination

It is therefore highly worthwhile to think about the state of mind of the people close to you, because you are under their influence just like they are under yours.

Most people are ruled by their Lower Nature and the forces of procrastination.

They may well be respecting official deadlines and not succumbing to the light side of procrastination. But in most cases they will be at the mercy of the far more insidious dark side of procrastination where there is no official deadline.

If that is the case for your friend, colleague or family member, then their ego is not going to like the fact that you are overcoming procrastination while they are not.

Your success is dangerous to their self-definition.

It wouldn't be so dangerous if you were someone they could dismiss as a distant superstar on a pedestal; it is the fact that you are a close acquaintance that makes it dangerous.

They know from years of experience that you are not all that different from them. So they can't claim that you were born with superhuman genes.

If you used to be like them, and now you have pulled yourself together and are making your dreams come true, then it follows that they could do it too if they would only channel their Deep Motivation and Take Action.

Their ego doesn't want them to face this truth, because to do so is painful. The pain may very well lead to them Taking Action, which would force their ego to revise its story about their identity.

It requires far less effort and pain for them to explain away your success.

This is why when you begin to make progress you will start hearing your friends, family members and colleagues saying that you are *lucky* or *talented*.

Or they might be less polite.

If you are Taking Action then you are a threat to the credibility of the stories that your friends, family members and colleagues are telling themselves in order to avoid Taking Action. So they have to discredit you in order to feel comfortable with their procrastination.

The good opinion of others

Abraham Maslow said that the first condition for becoming a self-actualised person is to be independent of the good opinion of others.

Remember the mirror neurons. Your consciousness is not isolated from that of the people around you. So you need to exert conscious effort in order to empathise less with the people who interpret reality in ways that lead you away from accomplishing your Great Work.

Do it anyway

William Blake said: "Listen to the fool's reproach; it is a kingly title." This is how you should take such negations of your efforts from people who are close to you or feel threatened by you for other reasons.

If you are Taking Action and are being reproached by someone who is not, you should take their reproach as a sign that you are doing the right thing. It is one of the earliest signs of success.

The praise, fame and money will usually come later – much later, in some cases. It can be hard to work for years without getting any positive feedback. So in the absence of anything else, take the reproaches from procrastinators as positive feedback, even if on the surface it looks like negative feedback.

Don't waste your energy reacting to what other people say about you. Don't get into arguments or other situations where you find yourself justifying your actions.

If you explain yourself to others then your energy will be drained from your work and go into defending the rightness of what you are doing.

If someone starts giving you advice or trying to make you justify yourself, then one thing you can do is to focus less on yourself. Give him or her your attention. Don't judge him. Just be conscious of how he feels and support him as well as you can without taking it personally. You will find that people are mostly just hungry for someone who listens to them, because usually no one listens to anybody.

In many cases, people will not insist on their criticism about you: all they really wanted was validation that what *they* are doing is OK. So give them your attention and validation, and then quietly get on with your Great Work.

Realise that people's reactions are not about you but about them. Try to help them if you can. But do not let anyone drag you down. Learn to recognise the labels used by envious people, see them for what they are, and don't allow yourself to be affected by them.

Here is a non-comprehensive list of labels that people might attach to you. I'm sure you can or will be able to add some of your own. The labels you will come up against will depend on your way of Taking Action, but the labels in the table on the following page are quite generic:

Label	Translation
You are "lucky"	Your labeller doesn't have to Take Action because he or she doesn't have that kind of luck.
You are "talented"	Your labeller doesn't have to Take Action because he or she doesn't have that kind of talent.
You are "lazy"	You look happy so you are obviously not working. Your success must be the result of luck or talent (see above).
You are an "egotist"	Your labeller isn't Taking Action because he or she is a better person than you. They don't believe in fulfilling their own dreams because they are focusing on the good of mankind. Like them, you should be doing something you don't want to do.

You should get a "real job"	Your labeller isn't Taking Action because he or she is a better person than you. They don't believe in fulfilling their own dreams because they are focusing on the good of mankind. Like them, you should be refusing the call of your Higher Nature and doing something you don't want to do.
What you are doing is "morally wrong"	Anyone who is taking proactive, concerted action to accomplish something must be stepping on other people's heads to get what they want. Your labeller is a better person than you and therefore doesn't have to Take Action. (However if you hear this a lot from many different people, you should probably take a close look at what you are doing, to make sure you are morally in the white.)
They have a monologue of "advice" they want you to listen to	Your labeller already knows all there is to know about what you are doing, even though they have never actually done it. So they don't have to Take Action.

Chapter 15

Your Own Jailer

"Slavery takes hold of few, but many take hold of slavery."

– Seneca

Now that we have talked about others, I want you to take what you have learnt and apply it to yourself.

After all, you are reading this book to help yourself, and not to be able to blame others with greater eloquence.

Who are you in the scenario described in the previous chapter? Are you the person who has started Taking Action and who is now being told that he or she is "lucky" or "talented", or anything else that negates his or her accomplishments?

If so, congratulate yourself. You are making real progress.

However, now is the time to take a hard look at yourself. It is easy to spot other people's unconsciousness, but one of the hardest things in life is to become conscious of our *own* unconsciousness. Could it be that *you* are blaming or sabotaging others for Taking Action or for being successful?

If you are reading this then you are probably working on improving yourself. You are taking proactive action in your life. If so, you are already ahead of most people. You are probably not addicted to gossip, envy or negativity. Or at least you are taking action to distance yourself from such behaviours.

However, the drive to bring other people down can manifest in very subtle ways, and it does require a lot of attention to completely avoid such behaviours.

It is important, however, because doing those things blocks you from accessing your Higher Nature.

As we have established, you can only accomplish your Great Work through your Higher Nature.

If you label and resent people who are Taking Action from their core, then the first person you hinder is not them but yourself.

The person who is Taking Action has overcome his or her own ego, so he can probably overcome yours as well.

If he has worked sufficiently on himself then he will remain unreactive to other people's labelling of him.

He will not spend his energy on drama, because his energy is reserved for his project of making his life and the world more beautiful.

So if you label and resent him for Taking Action, you are chiefly hindering your own ability to Take Action.

For your own sake, don't do it. Even if you *were* to succeed to drag a positive person down with your negativity, your victory would not bring you joy.

I know you have good intentions. My reasons for this tough love is that there are temptations lurking at every corner on this journey, and if you succumb to them they will subtly bring you down and prevent you from accomplishing your Great Work.

What we are really fighting is unconsciousness. It is easy to succumb to the illusion that other people's accomplishments are a threat. But that is just another excuse for not Taking Action.

The true victory is the victory over your own ego. That is the victory that brings you closer to accessing that critical mass of Deep Motivation that will absolutely make you Take Action in your own life.

Your ego definitions

Why do I say that the way to success is to overcome your ego?

At the first glance, it seems like a bizarre statement.

Isn't the ego all about success? Don't we usually associate it with achieving success in the external world and being proud of it?

There certainly is a degree of that going on. But the popular perception that the ego is all about self-praise is not the whole truth.

In fact, the ego is about any rigid self-definition, be it positive or negative.

"I'm a loser" is just as much of an ego definition as "I am the King of the World".

It *is* true that your ego is invested in the image that your successes have got you; however it is just as invested in the image that your *failures* have got you and the way that other people have defined you, especially in childhood.

So if you failed at a certain subject in school then your ego has probably created an identity out of how you're no good at that subject.

The reason you failed may well have been that you had an uninspiring teacher; if you had had a better teacher you may even have specialised in that subject and become an expert.

But now you have told yourself a story about how you're no good at that subject, and your ego is defending this story.

Likewise, if your parents told you that you would never amount to anything, then chances are your ego is invested in that image and will continuously sabotage your success until you learn to overcome its judgements.

If, on the other hand, everyone told you that you would grow up to be a big success, then your ego is probably invested in that image and has been spurring you on to success until the reality of your situation matched your ego's story about who you are.

At first sight it may seem like it's a huge advantage to have the kind of ego that tells you that you are a success by default.

I think that it is indeed an advantage in the beginning of your journey. However, it is still very limited because as long as you are relying on other people's definitions of you, you will be achieving what in their eyes is success and not necessarily that which is your heart's desire: your Great Work.

So your ego can set you up for failure or it can set you up for success. However, the success that it will allow you to have will be a certain kind of success that has been pre-determined by others – often your parents.

Such success is almost always accompanied or followed by an identity crisis.

True success, the success of fulfilling your Great Work, is antithetical to the ego.

It is when you *disconnect* from your ego that you get on with your work; it is when you ignore the mental chatter and self-definitions of the ego that you are able to Take Action.

That is when you make your big gains.

Your ego is never far behind you, however. It is constantly interpreting and judging the action you are taking and the results you are achieving.

Let's say you Took Action. You advanced to a higher level of accomplishment and consciousness. Now your ego has made an identity out of the success you achieved. It has revised its story about who you are, and this new story is holding you in your new place.

Without the resistance of your ego you would still be advancing. But now that your ego has made an identity out of your accomplishments, you're afraid of losing what you've got.

Without your ego you wouldn't be afraid. You wouldn't have a story to defend, so there would be no need for you to rest on your laurels. You wouldn't need to hold on to the idea of past successes but would go ahead and pursue new ones.

The ego is all about identity. When you are evolving and having new experiences, your ego is desperately grabbing for ideas about what these experiences say about who you are.

Most people live in the illusion that their identity is written in stone. However in reality your ego is constantly interpreting the events of your life and even those of the lives of the people around you in order to adapt your identity and make it look solid when cross-referenced with facts.

Your inner tormentor

Like almost everyone else, you probably have an inner dialogue or monologue going on inside your head.

This doesn't mean that you're crazy. It means that you're normal.

I should probably specify that I'm not talking about actually *hearing* a voice. That would be more of a psychiatric symptom or a hard-core spiritual experience.

What I'm talking about here is rather the inner thought stream that almost everybody has.

The "voice" in your head comes from your ego. As we have just discussed, the ego is all about identity; so the main occupation of this "voice" is to judge the events of your life in terms of what they say about who you are.

Often this "voice" is like the commentator of a sports match as it judges the events of your life and the actions you take. Just like such a commentator, it is usually completely superfluous: the events and actions take place regardless of the commentary; if you turned off the sound, you would still be seeing the same image.

Sometimes your inner voice will congratulate you on how great you are, and sometimes it will scold you for not being good enough. When it does the latter, it takes the form of what is referred to in mindfulness circles as the *inner tormentor*.

Your inner voice may be softly spoken, or it may be rude or aggressive.

In the following, I will offer some examples of what you might experience if you happen to have an aggressive inner tormenter. If you do not suffer from this kind of inner tormenter, I congratulate you. However, it can still be useful for you to read this section because it offers an insight into the structure of the ego.

I have to warn you that for the rest of this section there will be rude and aggressive language. So if you don't like that or are not in the mood for it, then please skip to the next section.

It is not that I like that kind of language; but I found it impossible to describe the inner tormentor without using some of its favourite words. This is important because if you have a rude inner tormentor, I want you to realise how normal this kind of toxicity is, and not feel guilty about it.

If you're not in the mood for foul language, then please skip to page 128, to the section entitled "Your inner toady".

Try to talk to someone you are nervous about talking to. Make the slightest awkward remark and your inner tormentor might tell you, "Why didn't you just keep your mouth shut you fucking idiot!"

The truth is that the mere fact you talked to that person is a big reason to congratulate yourself, no matter what slipped out of your mouth when you were understandably under stress. If you confronted your fears and followed your drive, then you took a major step in the right direction no matter how it panned out. You really deserve to give yourself props.

Your inner tormentor is scared you will discover that fact. So when you first step out of your comfort zone, it attacks you even more ferociously than usual.

It often also attacks you if you go to the opposite extreme.

If you are overweight and you wake up hung over and eat that ice cream you know is in your freezer, your inner tormentor will tell you you're a "fat cow" or a "fat slob". Or it might go further with "Lose some weight you bitch slut whore!"

One of the triggering factors of the inner tormentor at this point could be the low levels of the brain chemical serotonin that come with being hung over and/or coming off a sugar high.

However, if you do have a toxic inner tormenter, then there can also be something else at play: while it doesn't want to see you Taking Action to address your flaws, it doesn't want to see you accepting them either. It wants you right there in the middle, feeling guilty for not being "good enough".

It is interesting that the inner tormentor's expressions are often direct copies of those used by people who criticised you when you were a child.

This could be because at that time you interpreted those people as being important to your survival.

Your brain wants to keep you alive, so when your behaviour goes beyond what those people – parents, teachers, relatives – would have accepted, it echoes what they used to say to you to keep you in line. This is because nature made children receptive to the instructions of their elders on the assumption that these elders would impart the wisdom they accumulated in the course of their lives to help the children survive, thrive and grow into healthy adults. This may indeed have been the case for you if your caregivers were not pathological and therefore only limited your behaviour for positive reasons and in non-violent ways.

Unfortunately, this is not always the case.

There is something that can make your inner tormentor even more furious than when you eat that ice cream. Paradoxically, that is when you try to improve yourself and exert your willpower to *not* submit to temptation. When this happens, it might say: "You'll never manage to lose weight. You will always be a fat cow!" or whatever.

This is especially the case if your parents, siblings or caregivers were afraid that you would become more successful than them, and therefore taught you to be ashamed of your talents or beauty. In these cases, your ego will try to keep you under the sway of your Lower Nature so that you don't become too successful. This is at first because if you do break free from temptation, you will have to directly experience the pain of the shame that was programmed into you.

This shame is expressed verbally by the inner tormentor, which at this point can become insanely aggressive. However, if you manage to listen consciously, you can almost hear a note of desperation in its "voice". This is because it knows you are very close to breaking free of it.

Some favourite expressions of the inner tormentor are:

Fat, bitch, cow, slut, fucking loser, wanker.

Some people's inner tormentors can get so aggressive and persistent that they cause depression or even suicide.

So if your inner tormentor is just the run-of-the-mill judgemental "voice" that seeks to keep you within your comfort zone, you really have nothing to complain about.

No matter how bad your inner tormentor is, you should know that the key to overcoming it is to avoid identifying with it.

In our culture we are encouraged to regard any thoughts that we find in our own head as "our own."

This is partly because we are afraid to say or even think something that may be seen as a sign of being crazy.

We are very scared of that label. And for good reason: crazy people lose their family, their property and their good name. They are locked away and pumped so full of drugs that they live the rest of their lives as vegetables.

At least this is the popular view.

However, as many people have found, identifying with the thoughts of the inner tormentor can be a source of profound pain.

If a random person on the street were to call you an idiot and a loser, you might get momentarily upset, but you probably wouldn't take it to heart on the long term.

Rather, you would probably perceive it as saying more about him than about you.

"What a rude person," you would say, and move on without giving him another thought.

However, if you believe that you are calling *yourself* an idiot and a loser, and that you are repeating it several times a day, you might very well be opening yourself up to real hurt on the longer term.

Most of us are inhibited by our judgements of ourselves in one way or another. Most of us are held back from achieving our desires by our own limiting beliefs about who we are.

Those beliefs acquire an extra sting when they come from the rude mouth of the inner tormentor.

The good news is that these thoughts aren't really yours, but your ego's.

As I have repeated countless times, your ego wants to keep you in place; it doesn't want you to rise or fall too much too fast.

You can't really blame it: it is trying to keep you safe, in its own way.

However, the ego can behave like a bull in a china shop, destroying beautiful craftsmanship with each of its jerky moves.

There are safe ways by which you can overcome the limitations of your ego.

As you start applying the philosophy of this book, you will become more conscious of your own inner processes.

If you are one of the people for whom the ego takes the form of an inner tormentor, then try to observe yourself and notice when that inner voice shows itself the most and when it is harshest.

It probably often comes up when you have been engaging in activities that resonate with its negative energy, such as eating bad food, taking mind-dulling drugs, looking at social media or gossiping. It might be the case that you only hear its "voice" just after you leave those mentally noisy activities.

This is because while you are engaging in activities through your Lower Nature, the ego is strengthened but the inner noise is so high that even your ego becomes inaudible. So when you leave those activities and are on your own, the inner tormenter returns with a vengeance.

As mentioned, you will probably also find that it is very harsh when you are in a situation you are not accustomed to or comfortable with, trying to do something you have never done before. The ego knows you are trying to transcend its definition of you, so it is sabotaging you.

You have to learn to see this as positive feedback. It is a sign that you are doing the right thing.

Your inner toady

Then, when you manage to ignore the negative thoughts and succeed despite them, your ego will attack you from the opposite flank.

It will start telling you how *great* you are. For instance, let's say you are beginning to see your great project take shape. Your inner voice becomes jubilant and starts raving about the fame and fortune that is just around the corner.

This too is a trap, because it makes you underestimate your challenges and indulge in listening to the flattery of your inner toady. The "voice" of the ego can consume so great a part of your mental capacity that you are unable to focus enough on what is actually going on, so again you risk failure.

The Myth of Inspiration

One of the things that keeps a lot of people from doing any activity through their Higher Self is the Myth of Inspiration.

According to this myth, artists should only Take Action when inspiration strikes.

The myth says that artists spend their time wearing funky clothes, hanging out in cafes, travelling and getting high.

Then suddenly inspiration strikes and the artist takes out his notepad, easel or musical instrument and starts creating feverishly.

He soon finishes his work of art and returns triumphantly to his Bohemian life while "the suits" work out the details.

Making an effort is looked down upon. The myth says that "true artists" don't make an effort. The idea is that for something to be worth creating, it has to come straight from heaven.

The most prominent variations of this myth that I know of are the story of Sylvester Stallone hammering out the screenplay for Rocky in 20 hours straight and the story of how Jack Kerouac wrote *On the Road* in 20 days, with hundreds of sheets of paper taped together into a long scroll so he wouldn't have to spend time changing the paper in his typewriter.

I don't know how long it really took Sylvester Stallone to write the first draft of *Rocky*, but the screenplay went through nine "sizeable rewrites" before it was accepted (source: IMDB.com).

Jack Kerouac had written many versions of *On the Road* and had agonised over the story for three years before he entered the celebrated three-week frenzy in 1951 when he wrote the scroll.

Furthermore, after he did write the scroll, his publisher wouldn't accept it so he had to spend several years revising it. *On the Road* was published in 1957, nine years after Kerouac started work on the book, and six years after he finished the scroll.

Despite this, the myth about Jack Kerouac's writing *On the Road* in 20 days was actually promoted by his publisher as part of the publicity campaign when the book finally came out. This was because they knew it is the kind of myth that appeals to people.

This is again because the Myth of Inspiration supplies the perfect excuse for not Taking Action.

For the procrastinator, inspiration never strikes. Well, actually it does, but it never seems to come at that ideal time when the procrastinator feels like working. Or it doesn't seem to come often enough to create a consistent work.

The Jack Kerouac myth is the perfect excuse for laziness. The procrastinator says:

"I'm going to do my Great Work as soon as inspiration strikes the same way it did for Jack Kerouac. If inspiration doesn't come to me like that, it means I'm not meant to do anything yet."

The truth about inspiration is that it exists in limitless supply, and it's available to everyone. The universe is overflowing with inspiration. Everything in the universe is the result of inspiration. The universe *itself* is the result of inspiration. There is no shortage of inspiration. Lack of inspiration can never be an excuse for not Taking Action.

In fact, the more you Take Action the more inspiration becomes available to you.

I remember watching a documentary about the pop group Abba. One of the members said that writing a pop song was like waiting for a wild animal to come out of its cave.

You want to take a photo of it, but you can only do it when the animal happens to come out.

Failure Factors

Taking the photo will only take a few seconds. But you don't know when the animal will come out of the cave. So you have to stay there, waiting.

It's tempting to go and do something else, but if you're not there waiting outside the cave, you might miss the animal when it comes out.

In the same way, Taking Action has to come before inspiration. It's tempting to go and do something else, but if you're not Taking Action, you will miss the inspiration when it comes.

When I started writing my first book, I spent a long time not knowing how to write it. This made me procrastinate doing other things.

But then someone told me that if I wanted to finish the book I should set aside a certain time interval each day and sit down to write.

I followed her advice. I sat in front of the computer every day with the document open. At first I would spend some time doing nothing, convinced that I would have no usable ideas that day. But then, as I sat there, the words would start to flow.

Today, two novels later, as soon as I sit down in front of my document, inspiration starts spilling through my fingers.

Just like *On the Road* didn't come to Jack Kerouac out of the blue and get published the next day, I didn't start with a free flow of inspiration. On the contrary that flow was the result of countless battles with my own laziness and Lower Nature.

The point is to Take Action. As soon as you prove beyond doubt that you are serious about this, inspiration will offer itself to you.

Nihilism

At first when you set out to accomplish something big, your ego will send "information" and other sources of procrastination your way.

If you plough through these temptations, it will try to scare you with ideas that you are not good enough to do what you have set out to do – or that you are too good.

If you still insist, it might start getting really rude. It might start insulting you extremely aggressively.

If you ignore even that, it might then turn to existential reasons for not Taking Action. These may not be verbalised, but they are underlying. They are usually phrased something like this:

Imagine you do pull yourself together and spend years with your nose to the grindstone creating your masterpiece. What if the world ended before you were done? Wouldn't all that effort have been a waste? Wouldn't it have been better if you had spent that time "enjoying your life" and living for pleasure?

So what's the point? Why not just eat pizza and binge on torrented TV shows all day? Or smoke crack. Or stare at cat videos. Or gossip. We're all going to die anyway, no matter what we do. So why not kill time with pleasure and entertainment until time kills us?

This is the ego's nihilistic reasoning. It may not be telling you in so many words; it may instead be focusing on classical rationalisations for procrastination. But if you grab it by the throat and demand its existential reasoning, then this is what it will tell you.

The reason the ego thinks like this is because it functions through your Lower Nature. So it judges everything in terms of how much pleasure you will gain in exchange for how much effort.

Pleasure is great. I like pleasure. But what the ego doesn't know is that there is something far greater than pleasure. It is called happiness. The reason the ego doesn't know about happiness is that happiness is found only where the ego is not.

Part III

Take Action

Putting it all together to a recipe for Taking Action
on your Great Work, and becoming happier
and more conscious in the process.

Chapter 16

Take Action from Your Soul

"The most sublime act is to set another before you."

– William Blake

How do you overcome your ego's resistance to the success you are aiming for?

One important method that can help you circumvent your ego's sabotage is to accept success without insisting that it has to be "your" success.

At first this may seem counterintuitive because we are used to the idea that in order to obtain success you must focus on your own gains and get ahead of others.

However it is still true, and it is due to something that very few people know:

Unbeknownst to ourselves, deep down inside, beyond the noise of our egos, we are noble creatures.

You may not feel noble, or you may not feel that the people around you are noble. This is because in our noisy society we have grown unaccustomed to being connected with our soul.

Your soul is noble. It has no way of being otherwise.

Connect to that part of yourself and you won't need this book or any other book or person to give you advice.

Your soul doesn't understand the concept of success which exists only for "me". It doesn't put conditions on success, or on anything else for that matter.

The soul doesn't operate with that kind of complicated mental entanglements. For the soul, either there is success or there isn't. If you put a blockage on anybody's success through resentment or envy, then you communicate to your soul that you don't want it to manifest success.

If you are blocking success, you are blocking it for everyone including you.

In fact, if you are blocking success in any shape or form, you are chiefly blocking your own success.

After all you have greater influence over yourself than you have over anyone else.

So support other people's success.

You have a lot to gain from supporting your acquaintances' efforts to take right action and to accomplish their Great Work, even if you yourself aren't really Taking Action yet – in fact *especially* if you aren't really Taking Action yet.

By supporting other people's success, you open yourself up to success. That is a very important milestone.

Chapter 17

Support Other People's Success

"The greatest good you can do for another is not just to share your riches but to reveal to him his own."

– Benjamin Disraeli

If you are like most people then truly encouraging and wishing the best for another person will entail a major struggle with yourself. This is especially true if they are close to you and if they are more on their path than you are on yours.

I'm not saying that this is the case for you. However it is a common pattern that it is important to be aware of. So please bear with me for a few paragraphs.

It's easy to wish the best for someone who you don't really think is going to make it; it's much harder to wish the best for a friend who you suspect might do better than you.

It's easy to hear a famous person like Richard Branson's rags-to-riches story and find it "inspirational". But your *friend's* rags-to-riches story sounds more like your friend bragging. It can be hard to get over yourself sufficiently to see your friend's story as inspirational.

If you knew him or her before he made it, then you know he is only human. He's not special. Why is he bragging? It can be very difficult not to get annoyed.

Incredibly, this holds true even if your "bragging" friend is Richard Branson himself. This is because the criteria for finding a story inspirational is not only how impressive the *story* is, but perhaps even more *who* it comes from. Most people prefer the stories that come from someone they don't know personally.

This is once again because if you can make yourself perceive a successful person as cut from a different cloth than you, as if they didn't come from this dust and ashes that we all come from, then you have an excuse for not Taking Action.

Ironically, this means that the people who are too distant to inspire you to Take Action are the ones you are most likely to see as "inspirational". They are not a threat to your ego.

But then someone comes along whom you have known for several years as a normal human being, and *they* go and pull themselves together to Take Action.

When this person achieves success it is very tempting to say that he or she is "lucky" or "talented" or "kidding himself" or "a kid who doesn't know the realities of life" or "going through a midlife crisis" or "senile", or whatever.

If you do this then you are probably dodging the obvious question: why didn't *you* Take Action?

I'm not saying that you have to Take Action just because a friend is. What I'm saying is that since your ego interprets every event in terms of what it says about *you*, then this is the obvious question that will be on your ego's mind and which it will therefore attempt to studiously ignore.

Don't fall for the temptation to explain away someone else's success.

If you perceive someone as successful, and you want what they have, then don't complain about it or negate it.

If this person is actually Taking Action and producing results, then consider offering them your support. The world is full of negativity, drama and reaction-seeking. If you have a friend or family member who is actually building something based on their personal truth, and is not treating you horribly, then count yourself lucky. You have personal access to a role model.

Take Action

I remember the first time I became conscious that I had met someone who was Taking Action from his true core. His style was very different from mine, and since he was exposing his life so honestly to the spotlight he was supremely vulnerable. It was tempting to laugh at some of his idiosyncrasies that were so vulnerably exposed. However deep down inside I knew I had no right to laugh. Because he had found the courage within himself to Take Action and put himself forward, and I hadn't.

So I supported him wholeheartedly. I think this was an important step on my way to where I am today – living my dream doing what I want, living where I want and expressing what I want.

When I say that I am living my dream, it doesn't mean that everything is just rosy and easy.

It means that I am living the life I have chosen and that I'm fighting for the life that I choose.

However, a lot of people would not really want to live my life. They might not be willing to pay the price for freedom.

Yes, there is a price for freedom. At least in a sense there is a price for everything.

The price of freedom is usually less security.

If you see someone who has what you want, then help him. He may seem like a giant at first; but he is not some invincible icon. He is a courageous human being who could fail at any moment but perseveres regardless. When you help him on his beautiful mission, you start to partake of his courage. It enters you and supports you.

It is essential that you open yourself up to success by accepting it in others first.

Because, as I have demonstrated above, by not accepting success in other people you are not cutting them off from success; you are only getting in your own way.

Truly successful people are not "lucky"; they are people who let go of the notions of luck and talent and stop being offended by other people's success. Instead they channel their own Deep Motivation. They Take Action and learn Self-discipline.

Chapter 18

The Art of Manifesting

"Your job in this whole business of manifesting is not to say how or when, but just 'Yes'."

– Wayne Dyer

"I do what I love and I love what I do."

I looked at the post-it on my monitor as I sat down in front of my computer at work.

And just like every other morning, the words annoyed me. I didn't feel they were true at all. Part of me wanted to tear the yellow note from the monitor and throw it in the recycle bin.

However, I resisted the temptation. I had placed the note there as a conscious intention that I desperately wanted to manifest.

I was determined to either change my attitude to my job or change my job. I had seen many times how people can stay for years or decades in a situation that they don't like and continuously complain about it. I had seen how I was starting to become that person, and it frightened me.

Take Action

I was in a good and safe job with great conditions, and I couldn't see how I could summon the courage to leave it all behind. However I wanted to stop complaining. If I didn't have the guts to leave, then I wanted to be happy where I was. As a bare minimum I wanted to embrace it as a conscious choice.

I could see the danger of avoiding being conscious of my situation. I knew the symptoms of that predicament: to be complaining yet staying in the same place.

So I did what I could at that point: I stated my intention, despite the fact that I had no idea how it could come about.

As Wayne Dyer says in his *Manifesting Your Destiny* audio course, "Your job in this whole business of manifesting is not to say how or when, but just 'Yes.'" So I stated my intention and let go of the how and the when.

Every morning I would be confronted by my intention to do what I loved and love what I did. And every morning I felt how that intention didn't jive with reality.

As time passed it became obvious that I wasn't changing my attitude towards my job. And yet I wasn't denying it either; every morning I was reminded of the reality of the situation.

I am convinced that it was one of the things that eventually helped me push myself over the edge and Take Action.

Manifesting is when you set your intentions about what you want to accomplish. These intentions have to be expressed in a certain way with the right attitudes in place.

This book is not focused on the domain of setting intentions, because that is something that has been extensively covered by other self-development books.

As I'm sure you have noticed, it is focused on the domain of Taking Action.

However, I have dedicated this chapter to a quick treatment of the attitudes and principles for manifesting, because they are important. They are what guide the essential effort of Taking Action.

All of the following principles have been expressed in this book, albeit from the perspective of Taking Action, rather than of setting intentions and manifesting.

It is often useful to see things from a different perspective. So I have summed up the main points of manifesting below, as a list you can refer back to for reminders and troubleshooting.

Furthermore, if you already know the principles of manifesting from other books, this chapter will translate them for you into the principles of this book.

Now for a quick summary of the principles of manifesting. I will express them in the terminology of this book, which means that I will explain them slightly differently than most books on manifesting.

Setting intentions

The way to do it is to formulate your intentions as if they are already reality and then tune into the *feeling* of that reality.

Your intentions must be expressed in purely positive terms and in the present tense.

A great example is the one I used: "I do what I love and I love what I do."

This is a well-formulated intention because it transmits a positive state (love) and is expressed in the present tense as if the desire has already manifested.

The positive emotions put you in touch with your heart's desire and ultimately your Higher Nature; and the present tense helps the intention become reality because it is your soul that allows your intention to manifest, and your soul only knows the now.

A very badly formulated intention would have been: "I will be able to get out of my meaningless job as soon as I stop being terrified of the consequences."

Such an intention can't help you because it is loaded with negative emotion (meaningless, terrified) and is formulated in the future tense.

The negative emotions put you in touch with your fears and Lower Nature; and the future tense prevents you from moving forward because only the ego creates stories about the past and future.

The ego has no power of Manifestation, because it is not tapped into the source where the things you want to manifest come from.

Once you have written down some well-formulated intentions, you tune into the feeling that they exude.

Let's take our well-formulated intention from above:

"I do what I love and I love what I do."

Tune into that intention or any well-formulated intention of your own. Really feel it and meditate on the feeling.

Take Action

Once you have internalised the feeling of the intention, you won't need to remember the words, because whenever you tune into the feeling, you are in resonance with the manifestation of your intention.

However, if part of you is strongly resisting your intention, as was the case with me, because I was scared of the consequences, then it is a good idea to keep reminding yourself of your intention.

Put it somewhere you can't ignore it, just like I did.

Then get into the feeling of your intention.

The idea that has been expounded widely is that in connecting to the feeling of your intention you make yourself "resonate at the same frequency" as the things you want to manifest.

There is some truth to this statement, but the trouble is that it is unclear what it means.

So far no one has been able to measure the wavelength of the desire for specific goals, such as for a Ferrari or a life partner.

It is therefore more useful to formulate it in a different way.

In the terminology of this book we may say that when you write down your intentions it is probable that you will start out with desires that resonate most with your Lower Nature because that is probably where you are coming from at that point.

Positive thinking

This and many, many other books have established that thoughts have creative power. Thoughts create reality.

It follows that if you focus on the lacks that you may feel in your life and resentment towards other people and the world in general, then you will manifest the lack and multiply your reasons for feeling resentful.

The opposite is also true: if you focus on the abundance of your life and the gratitude you feel, then more abundance and more reasons for gratitude will manifest.

So live through your Higher Nature. Focus on what you want, not on what you don't want.

Disconnecting from the outcome

It is essential to maintain this positive attitude even when things are not working out the way you imagined.

After all, your imagination about your success or failure all comes from your ego.

As explained earlier in this book, the ego is a collection of ideas about who you are.

Your soul, on the other hand, is all about reality. It is about seeing what actually *is*.

We tend to think that all this manifestation stuff is fantasy, and that our little ego concerns are "reality". The opposite is true.

It is like the story about David Barrier in Chapter 3: "Your Soul".

David Barrier was so caught up in his ego fantasy about being a great driver and navigator that he completely ignored the reality of Los Angeles.

He had never been to Los Angeles, and he didn't have the open-mindedness to allow anything to exist that he didn't know about already.

He was so attached to the outcome that he couldn't allow anything to manifest that he didn't know all the details about.

Obviously, if you want new experiences, new things in your life, then by definition you can't expect to know everything about them in advance. You can't insist on controlling every little detail of their manifestation. Because if you do, you are really insisting on only manifesting things that you already have.

So you have to let go and disconnect from your ego's stories about how things need to be.

And you have to let go of the negative interpretations of reality that your ego spouts when it doesn't get things exactly as it imagined.

As we have discussed, you can't allow your ego to get you into a negative or judgemental headspace. You have to keep your positive thinking in place even when things don't happen the way you imagined. You've got to allow your manifestation desires to show up in unexpected ways.

Take Action

Taking responsibility

When you disconnect from the outcome you open yourself up to the unexpected. This means that you don't judge reality.

When you stop judging reality, you begin to embrace it for what it actually is.

This is when you acquire the ability to take responsibility for the world and your life.

Taking responsibility is a very exciting step, because once you take responsibility for your life, you gain the ability to change it.

A good example of this is health. If you suffer from a health condition, then you gain the power to change it once you take responsibility for it.

As long as you are hanging onto an ego story that says your health shouldn't be the way it is, you block yourself from changing it.

However, when you see your health as it is, you gain the power to change it.

The reasons are simple:

If what you are looking at is your ego story, then you will only be able to change your ego story.

On the other hand, if what you are looking at is reality, then you are able to change reality.

This is why you have to take responsibility for your own life, including any ill health that you may be suffering.

Even if some things happened to you in your childhood that you now think about with sadness, you have to take responsibility for them.

Even if you could easily make the case that it was somebody else's fault, you still have to take responsibility.

Whatever happened then is in the past. This is now. You have to take responsibility for the way you are feeling and thinking *now*, and how it is affecting the accomplishment of your Great Work and thus your happiness.

Feeling worthy

If you want to manifest something into your life and you don't feel worthy of it, then one good piece of advice is to take a hard look at your life.

Since you are taking responsibility for your life as it actually is, you have to take responsibility for making it a life where you can imagine the presence of the thing you want to manifest.

For example, if your life is a complete mess then you probably can't imagine that your perfect life partner would be happy in your life. So that might be a reason for not feeling worthy of the perfect life partner.

One thing you can do is to think of a person who you feel would be worthy of having what you want. Then think about what it is about them that makes you feel that they are worthy. Then copy that aspect and make it your own. Be like them in that respect and you will allow yourself to have what you want.

For this to work, it is important that you accept the person's worthiness. This is what I talked about in Chapter 17: "Support Other People's Success".

If you resent other people's success, you cut yourself off from the success they are enjoying. However, if you support their success you can partake in it.

Although that is a powerful step, ultimately the most powerful thing you can do in the field of worthiness is to disconnect from your ego's need to label people as "worthy" or "unworthy".

In reality you are always worthy. You were born worthy, and no matter what has happened in your life since then, no matter what you have done or not done, you are still worthy.

It is the ego stories about who you are that make you define yourself as worthy or unworthy. Disconnect from those stories and you will realise your natural worthiness.

It sounds simple, but it is a goal that can take years to accomplish.

One thing that can accelerate this process is meditation.

Meditation

Practising meditation is like going to the spiritual gym.

It is repetitive, but on the longer term it increases your level in all the disciplines discussed in this book.

Countless meditation techniques are being taught these days, and it would be impossible to talk about all of them.

However, on the specific point of manifesting your desires in your life, I would encourage you to try

Take Action

Wayne Dyer's meditation from his book, *Manifesting Your Destiny*.

It's impossible to do that book justice in just a few lines, but here is a short outline of the meditation itself. The technique is simple:

You sit in whatever meditation pose you choose and focus on the things you want to manifest. You tune in to the feeling of them and chant the mantra, "Aaa".

Do this every morning.

When I started practising this meditation, I noticed a profound change. It was like already having what I wanted. It made me leave my house in the morning with deep happiness flowing through my body. It meant that when the things that I wanted to manifest did show up, I was open and receptive to them, and ready to accept them into my life.

Doing this meditation won't make your Great Work fall into your lap all done and dusted; you still have to work hard.

However, it will keep you on track and make it so much easier to keep Taking Action consistently.

There is a second part to this meditation: in the evening, remembering the events of the day and seeing how they resonated with the intentions you expressed in your morning mediation, focus on your gratitude for them and chant the mantra "Ohm".

It is important to do both the morning and the evening meditation, because manifestation is a cyclical process of intention and gratitude.

Practise the manifestation meditation every morning and evening for a couple of weeks and notice what starts to happen.

Doing this meditation has given me some amazing experiences of coincidences that were not coincidences. This is called serendipity.

Serendipity can be your friend all your life if you keep putting your intentions out there and Taking Action to accomplish your Great Work.

My theory about why this meditation works is that the focus on your manifestation desires and the chanting somehow burns away the ego stories about why you can't accomplish what you want. The meditation makes you see your manifestation desires as reality, and you tune into the happiness of their accomplishment. As you practise this meditation, you live increasingly through your Higher Nature and thus have direct access to your soul, which is tapped into the source of the things you want to manifest.

Gratitude

In the audio lecture course of *Manifesting Your Destiny*, Wayne Dyer tells the joke of a woman walking on the beach with her little grandson.

Suddenly a massive wave appears and carries her grandson out into the water.

Naturally, she is overcome by shock. She falls to her knees, sobbing.

"Oh dear God," she cries. "I beg you, bring my grandson back to me. I'll do anything. Oh dear God just please let him live!"

Suddenly, a new wave appears and drops her grandson back down beside her. She looks at him intently, drying her tears. He's perfectly all right.

Then she turns away and complains to God:

"Actually, he was wearing a hat..."

The grandson, not the hat

That was a joke, of course. However, the thing that makes jokes funny is how close they are to the truth.

We are often given more than we think; and we have less reason to complain than we believe.

What would have happened if the lady had thrown her grandson back into the water and refused to take him back unless he was returned with his hat on?

Wouldn't that be crazy?

And yet this is what so many of us do, every day of our lives.

The sane thing to do is to receive your grandson back with gratitude, and then buy him a new hat.

Chapter 19

Self-Discipline

"I'm just paying my rent every day in the Tower of Song."

– Leonard Cohen

When you start out on a path and formulate your intentions properly, things start to happen that feel almost like magic.

It feels like the universe is on your side. It feels like a confirmation that you are on the right path. And very likely, it *is* a confirmation.

The trouble is that in most people this fuzzy spiritual feeling leads to complacency. Since the human brain is wired for laziness by default, if you feel that the going is easy you will probably feel tempted to go easy yourself.

This is a trap, because the support that you receive at the beginning of your journey is not unconditional; the universe is encouraging you to double your efforts, not to slack off.

It's like downloading an app and having the premium version for free for the first month. If you don't pay for the premium version before the expiration of the trial period, you should not be surprised if after a month you no longer have access to the premium version.

On the surface it seems to make sense to only go for the freebies. Paradoxically, however, your life can become far richer if you pay for some things. The premium version is not limited to a month. All you have to do is pay a small amount and keep paying it.

Again, this doesn't sound like fun. We have been raised to prefer the free ride.

But I can tell you, it's an amazingly good deal. You can keep having the little coincidences on your side for the rest of your life as long as you continue to reward them with your wholehearted labour.

Furthermore, when you Take Action wholeheartedly, it becomes its own reward. You gain happiness from Taking Action on your Great Work, and you become a stronger and more consistent person in the process.

From intention to reality

Once your intentions are formulated and your manifesting is up and running, you have to then Take Action and do the heavy, repetitive lifting that will transform your Great Work from a well-formulated intention to solid reality.

In order to achieve this you have to cultivate self-discipline.

We have established that people who manage to channel their Deep Motivation and Take Action do not do so due to luck or talent.

They are able to Take Action because they have mustered enough self-discipline to barrel through the wall of procrastination.

Therefore, it is not luck or talent but self-discipline that is the true philosopher's stone.

The obstacles to self-discipline

The ego doesn't like self-discipline. The ego likes "talent" and "luck".

The ego likes stories about how someone was born with a silver spoon in their mouth or how the Illuminati or Freemasons or whoever are controlling us.

In reality the controllers behind the scenes are our own egos.

Take Action

Your ego has a complete protocol by which it seeks to prevent you from Taking Action.

"Eat that junk food," your ego tells you, knowing that it will take you away from the focus you need in order to Take Action. "You deserve it."

The insidious thing is what happens to your unconscious interpretation of reality if you consistently give in to your ego's temptations and threats instead of Taking Action.

"If it is true," you think, "that I *deserve* to eat a synthetic, rancid product and to wash it down with a carcinogenic soft drink that is so acidic it can be used to disinfect a toilet, then it must be because I'm not being me. I'm not living my purpose. I have no real reason to be alive and healthy."

"Now, now," your ego says. "That may be true. But there are ways to sweeten your existence."

"Jerk off to that porn video," it tells you. Or: "Watch that soap opera."

"Yes," you think unconsciously. "I might as well. My passion will never manifest in reality, anyway. I might as well go for the consolation prize of cheap titillation."

"Look at this person's vacation photos," your ego says.

"Yes," you think unconsciously. "I will never achieve what she has, so I might as well live vicariously. Oh, look at her on the beach eating lobsters with her boyfriend. She doesn't deserve that. It should have been me. She's so lucky. I've never been lucky."

My dear reader. I must confess that I feel physically sick after writing the above lines.

There was a time when to a certain extent I had a similar attitude. But now that I know how harmful this frame of mind is, I find it sickening to re-enter, even for the few minutes it took me to write.

Getting over the obstacles

"OK, so how do you get over yourself?" you might ask me. "How do you overcome your ego?"

There is no easy answer to that one.

However it is fundamental to remember that – as previously mentioned – the ego is all about identity. So if you can let go of your rigid self-definition, you are on the right path to Taking Action.

Take Action

This is logical because if the action that you want to take leads you to a new life situation, then it will mess with your current story about yourself. Your ideas about what you can and cannot achieve will change radically, and your ego is trying to prevent that.

You must disconnect from whatever your ego is telling you. You must uphold a positive attitude regardless of what your ego throws at you. Be aware of how it attempts to sabotage your success.

The most important thing is to put your head down and actually do the work that may get you where you want to go.

Yes, I said "may". It is a short word but it creates great discomfort. Your ego will exploit this discomfort to the full extent of its potential.

There are no guarantees that if you do the right thing you will get the outcome you desire. So be ready for some inner dialogue about how all the effort you are putting in "may" be for nothing.

One thing is guaranteed, however:

If you persist in doing the right thing despite any and all discouragement, you will become a far stronger, far more capable and mature person.

This is guaranteed, regardless of whether your project succeeds or not.

Tell your ego about this guarantee when its discouragement is close to making you give up all hope. The ego craves guarantees and finds it very hard to argue against them.

As you persist in your self-discipline you will make advances that you could not have achieved in any other way.

"Sure," your ego says, recovering. "All this hard work is fine for other people. But what is the shortcut? What is the five-step method that you can go through in a nice workshop to *eliminate* the problem once and for all?"

Your ego wants to sell you the delusion that there is a magic bullet that will kill your problem, just like antibiotics are thought to be a magic pill against bacteria. Your ego knows that as long as you keep clinging to the hope of a magic pill you will never take back control.

A similar delusion that it might feed your unconscious mind is that yes, indeed other people have to work hard, but *you* are a special case, and God (or the universe) has a special plan by which you will achieve what you want without being subjected to the inconvenience of having to Take Action.

You probably don't think this *consciously* – almost no one would persist in such a ludicrous belief if they stopped and thought about it.

And yet divine dispensation and magic pills sell like hot cake.

Everyone wants the magic pill. The trouble is that it doesn't exist. Indeed, if it did exist it would be a true contradiction in terms: short-term effort that leads to long-term success. An ordinary method that produces extraordinary results. It just doesn't add up.

So what *does* add up? You guessed it: long-term effort that creates long-term success.

That is a scary idea for most people.

It doesn't sound pleasant. It doesn't sound like something that would allow them to stay in whatever routine is holding them back and allowing them to feel comfortable and secure.

If you are like most people, then you probably can't see yourself taking incremental action over several years to achieve a long-term goal, no matter how much you would like to achieve it.

If this is the case for you, you shouldn't worry: no one was born with self-discipline.

Self-discipline is something you have to cultivate. This is done by repeatedly doing the right thing.

The best thing you can do is to Take Action on your Great Work every day, regardless of the obstacles that arise.

Chapter 20

Build Focus through Meditation

*"Meditation is like a gym in which you develop
the powerful mental muscles of Calm and Insight."*

– Ajahn Brahm

Take Action on your Great Work every day, and you will have good chances of succeeding.

This is a simple recipe, but it usually isn't easy.

Some extra power for dealing with the obstacles can be very useful.

Meditation is the most effective daily practice that I know for increasing and maintaining mental clarity.

A high level of consciousness is crucial in the effort to live through your Higher Nature. Meditation will help give you that.

There are many different kinds of meditation. I know a few of them quite well, and can talk about them from personal experience.

Take Action

One type of meditation that is focused on sharpening the mind and bringing about a high level of mental clarity is a kind of Buddhist meditation called Samatha.

In Samatha meditation, the main practice is to focus on one object. This is usually the breath, but it doesn't have to be: the important point here is to keep the mind on one object.

When you manage to focus on one single object, your mind becomes still, and you begin to feel deep happiness.

This is the exact opposite effect to when you expose yourself to "information", causing your mind to jump from object to object and exhaust itself.

If you have tried to practise Samatha meditation or any other kind of meditation where you focus on one object, you know how violently your mind rebels when you start out.

You sit down to meditate and immediately you feel an itch somewhere on your body that you feel you *must* scratch; or you have obsessive thoughts about something, which draw you away from your meditation object; or you feel extremely bored; or you get a strong urge to get up because you have too many things to do and you "really can't be sitting here any longer doing nothing."

What all these forms of resistance have in common is the mind's urge for stimulation.

It is when you let go of stimulation that your mind grows strong. Your consciousness grows and you achieve the level of consciousness necessary to accomplish your Great Work.

The two minds in Buddhism

The Buddhist monk and meditation teacher Ajahn Brahm is one of the foremost proponents of Samatha meditation in the world today. In one of his discourses he quotes his master, Ajahn Chah, who said that that if you want to have a strong body then you need to train your body; but if you want to have a strong mind you need to give your mind a rest.

This, Ajahn Brahm says, is due to the two minds in Buddhism, known as the Doing Mind and the Knowing Mind.

The Doing Mind is always labelling and judging. If your mind is jumping from object to object, labelling everything, then the Doing Mind has completely taken over and there is no room for the Knowing Mind.

If your Doing Mind has completely taken over, then all you see in the world will be your own labels.

Take Action

We are mostly a mixture of the Doing and Knowing minds. Most of us are able to live in the moment once in a while and really listen to someone or experience nature. However, in almost all people in our culture, the Doing Mind is vastly dominant.

This is why when you start out on your meditation career and sit down and focus on the breath, your mind immediately labels the breath.

"This is the breath. Big deal. What's for dinner?" it might say. Then it proceeds to jump from subject to subject.

However, you keep bringing your mind back to the breath. At one point, your mind starts to let go of its labelling of the breath. This is because when you give yourself time to look at one thing, your labelling of that thing begins to dissolve and you start to see it in depth. The Doing Mind starts to recede and the Knowing Mind takes its place. This is when you begin to experience reality on a deeper level. This is when you gain the ability to accomplish something meaningful in the world.

A very simple, essential and effective instruction for practising Samatha meditation is to keep your mind on the breath and enjoy taking a break from thinking.

If you catch yourself thinking, don't beat yourself up over it, because that entails more thinking. Just return your focus to the breath.

Don't focus on the breath in a particular place in the body. Don't worry about sitting in the "right" meditation posture, whatever that is.

Ajahn Brahm says in one of his discourses about meditation that the only thing that is important about your meditation posture is the corners of your mouth: they should be pointing upwards.

Smile. Meditation is the time when you get to take a break from thinking. It is in silence that you tune into your Higher Nature and the way to actually do your Great Work becomes clear.

Chapter 21

Actually Doing It

*"The journey of a thousand miles
begins with a single step."*

– Lao Tzu, *Tao Te Ching*

In this chapter I will give you some practical methods by which you can get over the resistance and noise and consistently chip away at your Great Work until you accomplish great things.

The following recipe sums up the core message of this book in nine practically applicable numbered points:

1. Tap into your Higher Nature

2. Manifest your desires

3. Take Action

4. Prioritise important over urgent

5. Avoid mind-dulling drugs, alcohol and junk food before and whilst Taking Action

6. Cut off "information" while Taking Action

7. Ignore ego chatter

8. Leverage your Lower Nature

9. Take a break.

Let's go over these points one at a time.

1) Tap into your Higher Nature

This is more of a principle than a step. It is the solid foundation that will help you throughout the process.

Almost no one acts from their Higher Nature all the time. I'm not demanding that you do that.

However I do recommend that you cultivate your Higher Nature and become conscious of the fact that you Take Action on your Great Work when you tap into your Higher Nature, and that you succumb to obstacles when you live through your Lower Nature.

You're still a blend of your Higher and Lower natures; but now you're conscious of which nature you are manifesting at any given moment and you know when and how you really need to cultivate your Higher Nature in order to actually carry out your Great Work.

2) Manifest your desires

Once you tap into your Higher Nature, you access your Deep Motivation by default because your Deep Motivation is the motivation of your Higher Nature to pursue your Great Work.

However if you are like me and most other people, you will do it in the opposite order: you start by accessing your Deep Motivation and this way discover your Higher Nature.

It is common to do it in this order because, as mentioned, most of us start out by focusing on what we can *get* rather than on what we can contribute.

If this is where you are coming from, then start by manifesting your desires, as described in chapter 18.

You start fulfilling your desires, and as your wishes begin to come true, you continuously update your list of intentions. At one point you will notice that increasingly the desires you express are aligning themselves with your Higher Nature. They are shifting towards your Great Work.

This is because as you start fulfilling your desires you peel away the layers of desire like the layers of an onion, from the most superficial to the most essential. You move from your superficial motivation to your Deep Motivation.

You will know when you start accessing your Deep Motivation, because at that point you will feel a profound longing to accomplish something that goes beyond yourself and is more important to you than the practicalities of your life.

In my case, I was in a very cushy job and I owned an apartment. When I was struck by Deep Motivation, it tempted me to quit my job, sell my apartment and set off on my quest of writing and exploring the world.

The thought scared me, and yet I couldn't let it go.

If you feel the same way about something, you might just be accessing your Deep Motivation.

When that happens, it will be time to pursue your Great Work. Time to Take Action.

3) Take Action

Set aside some time each day to work on your Great Work. Make it your first priority. Even if you are extremely busy at your day job, you can still set aside some time.

Even if you can only set aside half an hour, that half hour is extremely valuable. You will be amazed at what you can accomplish in half an hour if you focus completely on your task and don't let anything else into your headspace during that time. Further on in this section I will give you some techniques on how to focus and cut out the distractions.

Even if you think you aren't "inspired" on a certain day, still do it. Go to the place where you do your Great Work and stay there for the amount of time you have allocated.

If you do this, you will be surprised. The inspiration you thought wasn't there, will start flowing. You will discover that inspiration is in unlimited supply as long as you commit to it.

4) Prioritise important over urgent

Your Great Work is extremely important. However you will always be tempted to prioritise less important things.

This is one of the main points in Steven Covey's best-selling work, *The Seven Habits of Highly Successful People*.

Covey writes that there are four kinds of tasks, namely those that are:

1. Important and urgent;

2. important and non-urgent;

3. unimportant and urgent;

4. unimportant and non-urgent.

Intuitively we would assume that the important tasks would be prioritised. This is not the case, however. Almost everyone prioritises the *urgent* tasks.

This means that important non-urgent tasks are deferred in favour of unimportant but urgent tasks.

It is the same point as I made in Chapter 10: "The Dark Side of Procrastination", but it bears repeating.

It is very likely that someone will nudge you to complete tasks that will help them make money. They will usually set hard deadlines for you. Those tasks then become urgent for you.

Someone may even nudge you to complete a task that will help them accomplish their Great Work. If so you are lucky because it's a powerful thing to help someone accomplish their Great Work.

However, it is even more powerful to accomplish your own Great Work. And it is a rare friend indeed who nudges you to accomplish that. Most people live their entire life without ever meeting such a Rock.

So most likely the things that are important for you, but not for other people, never become urgent.

This is why there is a very real risk of postponing your Great Work to your deathbed.

It is crucial that you make yourself aware of this fact in time.

Set aside time each day for your Great Work. When more urgent things appear that tempt or pressure you to put off your Great Work till "tomorrow", remember that only you can make the decision to Take Action on your own mission.

5) Keep your mind clear

Now that you have made the time for your Great Work, and you are Taking Action, you have already got further than most people will ever get.

However now is the time to make sure you are Taking Action effectively.

Take Action

You must avoid putting anything into yourself that dulls your focus.

I know how puritanical this sounds.

I am not a puritanical person in regular life, but when I'm doing my Great Work I am highly conscious of the Failure Factors that lurk behind every corner.

When it comes to doing your Great Work, you're in a war to the death: either you do it (life) or you don't (death). Only you can make that call.

As already mentioned, no one is going to do this for you. In other areas of life you can get away with being sloppy because you can rely on someone else to take the lead; but when it comes to your Great Work, the responsibility is yours alone.

Treat the time you have set aside for your Great Work as sacred. Even if you only have a short amount of time to actually work on it each day, it will help you greatly if you structure your day around this time, making sure that your body is stocked up on healthy food and your mind is clear and ready to work.

When someone tells you to eat junk food "just this once" before or at a time when you should be working, just say no.

They might not understand you because they too are working, and *they* can eat junk food and still do their work; but your work is different. It requires your full focus because you alone are in charge and are giving your full gift.

When someone tells you to smoke a joint or get drunk "for inspiration" at or before a time when you should be working, be conscious of what that would cost you in terms of accomplishing your Great Work.

Outside of that time, go for it if you really want to or need to. But when you step into your creative space, your mind should be clear.

Forget about "inspiration". It's a myth for excuse-makers who want to avoid Taking Action.

6) Cut off "information"

At the time when you are Taking Action on your Great Work, you should cut off "information" as much as possible.

If there is part of your work that you can do without internet access, then it will help you to start with that part.

Put your phone and laptop on flight mode before starting.

That way you can't go onto social media or news sites or perform any other kind of internet procrastination during the time that you have set aside for your work.

If you feel that your willpower is low, you can switch off your modem if you're at home. If you feel you need to take tougher measures then unplug your modem completely and put it in a place where you would have to make an effort to get at it.

However, there are probably many tasks in the accomplishment of your Great Work where you do need internet access. When pursuing these tasks, there are measures you can take to avoid getting overwhelmed by online "information".

If you need to search for something online, make sure you only have tabs open that are connected to the information you are searching for.

If you need to post something on social media, do just that. Post whatever it is you need to post and then get the hell out of there.

Don't let yourself be tempted by the posts of others. Don't even look at them. You may well feel that your state of mind is so good that you can get away with clicking a button and looking at something without losing your clarity. Perhaps it's an interesting-looking article that you rationalise will help you in your Great Work.

However, the longer you stay in the social media environment exposing yourself to that level of consciousness, the more your Lower Nature will be awakened and will start demanding the things it likes, such as gossip and entertainment.

Before you know it all the time you set aside for pursuing your Great Work that day has vanished. And not only that – you may well have an unexplained urge to drink alcohol or eat unhealthy food, since those things resonate with gossip and cheap entertainment.

Post your stuff and don't listen to the siren song of all the things that social media will tempt your Lower Nature with. Get out of there as quickly as you can and continue Taking Action.

7) Ignore ego chatter

When you take the steps described above, you are truly Taking Action. You are on your way to making a radical change in your life.

You have overcome a major hurdle. However, you are not out of the woods just yet. The monsters of the forest have heard your forceful footsteps and are coming to intercept you.

Your Taking Action has caused panic. The egos of you and many other people will try to stop you, because you are threatening their world view.

Some people may try to discourage you by convincing you that your actions are irrational or risky.

Others may create drama or get sick.

Your own ego may tell you that there's no point in making an effort because you're never going to make it anyway. Or it may tell you that you've already made it so you don't have anything to prove. It will tell you anything to make you stop.

Things will appear that are more urgent (though less important) than your Great Work.

There will be no shortage of arguments, bribes or threats to make you stop Taking Action on your Great Work.

There is only one right thing to do in the face of all this distraction:

Ignore it and plough ahead.

8) Leverage your Lower Nature

As we have seen, your ego tends to get in the way of your Great Work. Your ego is governed by your Lower Nature, which resonates with stimulation and doesn't resonate with your Great Work.

Your Lower Nature is extremely powerful, so instead of opposing it head on, you can leverage it in the service of your Great Work.

Your Lower Nature chases pleasure and runs from pain. It chases the stimulation of immediate gratification and isn't motivated at all by the prospect of long-term accomplishment through delayed gratification.

So what you need to do is show your Lower Nature that it will feel pleasure when it works for your Great Work, and that it will feel pain when it opposes it: teach your Lower Nature that it will get immediate gratification from supporting your delayed gratification.

There are a variety of ways of doing this. For instance, you can set yourself up for ridicule if you don't follow through on your intentions.

Once you make a firm commitment with yourself, tell people about it. Then if you don't do it, your image will suffer. However make sure to only do this with people you know would support your project.

Otherwise all the energy would go into convincing them that your project is good and realistic instead of into upholding your resolution. In other words it would go from the soul to the ego.

Another method is a system of fines. I practise this with two like-minded friends who are my accountability partners. As far as I know, we are the first to do this.

The method is like this: we each have an Excel sheet that we fill in every day. On the horizontal axis are the things we are committed to doing or refraining from doing each day. On the vertical axis are the days of the month.

Each day we fill out a row. In each cell we note if we respected a given commitment that day.

Each commitment that we fail to respect on a given day results in us paying a fine to the others. At the end of the month we settle accounts. The persons with the highest numbers of fines pay the difference to the others.

We have been using this system for the last three years, and all of us estimate that we have accomplished far more than we would have if we hadn't been doing it.

The reason it works is that long-term success is achieved incrementally. What this means is that it is the little things you do consistently that make a huge difference over the long term.

So you need to be supremely conscious of the little things that you have to do every day to achieve your goal. The reason most people don't do these small tasks is that they are controlled by their Lower Nature. The Lower Nature only cares about instant gratification. Since there are no instant, spectacular consequences of doing or not doing these small tasks, it regards them as onerous.

One very easily understandable example of incremental achievement would be in the area of health. If you set yourself the little daily task of not smoking, then whether you respect it or not may not mean so much over the course of a week, but over the course of several decades it can determine the difference between healthy life and painful death. And yet your Lower Nature doesn't care. It prefers the sensations it gets from smoking, because they are instantaneous.

However, imagine if the price of cigarettes were to go up so much that each individual cigarette would cost 10 dollars. Now (depending on your finances) there may be instant consequences to smoking. Now your Lower Nature stops pestering you to smoke, firstly because smoking would mean having to work a lot to make more money and secondly because your Lower Nature realises that with that amount of money you could buy it something that would give it more pleasure than cigarettes.

So make sure there are instant consequences: if you don't do your tasks, you lose money; if you do your tasks more than your accountability partners, you gain money. That is language your Lower Nature understands.

Money is just an example. Perhaps there is something that will work better for you. The point is that you leverage the pain/pleasure mechanism of your Lower Nature to work for you.

You can even do this unilaterally. If you don't know anyone who is committed enough to be your accountability partner in the way described above, simply tell a friend that you will pay him or her, or do something for him, every time you don't keep your promise to yourself.

Or give the money to a beggar. This is equal to taking it from your Lower Nature and giving it to your Higher Nature, because you are doing something for someone other than yourself. Whomever you give it to, make sure to get rid of the money quickly so the pain is as instantaneous as possible.

Yes, I said pain. As we have seen in this book, doing your Great Work is serious business. It is supremely satisfying, but it isn't the path of pleasure. You have to face pain. This is the true meaning of the widely used expression of "leaving your comfort zone".

9) Take a break

Now that I have spent an entire book telling you to Take Action, I have to also tell you that once in a while it is important to take a break.

When you are truly Taking Action, a break can be something that can really help you get the results you are going for.

Archimedes' bath

One of the prime examples of this is the story about the Ancient Greek scientist, Archimedes of Syracuse.

A crown had been made for King Hiero II, who had supplied the pure gold to be used. The King asked Archimedes to determine whether some of the gold had been substituted with silver by the dishonest goldsmith.

Archimedes had to solve the problem without damaging the crown, so he could not melt it down into a regularly shaped object in order to calculate its density.

At that time it was not known how to determine the volume of an irregularly shaped object. Archimedes thought about the problem day and night, but didn't come up with a solution. After many days he decided to take a break and have a bath.

As he got into the tub, he noticed that the water level was rising. In a moment of epiphany he realised that this effect could be used to determine the volume of the crown.

Archimedes was so excited by having finally solved the problem that he ran out onto the street, naked as he was, crying "Eureka!" which in Ancient Greek means "I have found it!"

I'm not telling you to run around naked. However every part of the story about Archimedes is significant, including the part about his nakedness.

Archimedes was so engrossed in the problem he was trying to solve that when he finally found the solution he thought of nothing else, not even whether he was dressed or not.

And yet it was when he was taking a break that he found the solution. Sometimes the mind needs you to take a bath so it may access the silent space from which the solution can appear.

Afternoon tea

Then there is the apparently factual anecdote of the British army in Burma during World War II.

A small company of British soldiers were walking through the jungle when their scouts reported that they had wandered into a large battalion of Japanese soldiers.

The Japanese didn't know that the British were there, but the British soldiers were completely surrounded by the Japanese, so it was only a matter of time before they would come head to head.

Upon hearing the news some of the soldiers said, "Let's fight them. At least we will take as many of them with us when we die. We will have the element of surprise if we attack right now."

However their captain refused to give the order. Instead he instructed that tea should be brewed and that all soldiers sit down on the jungle floor and take their afternoon tea.

This was the British army, after all.

It is not hard to imagine the state of unease with which some of the soldiers probably held their tea cups. However, orders were orders, so they kept a stiff upper lip and drank their tea quietly, right there on the jungle floor.

During the tea break the scouts returned to report that the Japanese had moved and now there was an opening in their lines. The British could slip away and escape.

This was how a tea break saved the lives of an entire company.

Again, notice the tension between a very high level of Taking Action and taking a break.

Ananda's enlightenment

Ananda was the Buddha's attendant. He stayed with him and served him for 25 years. Many other monks who had far less contact with the Buddha became enlightened during this time. However at the time of the Buddha's death, Ananda had still not attained nirvana.

After the Buddha's death, the First Buddhist Council was arranged. Everybody invited to attend the

Council were already enlightened, except for Ananda. Not wanting to be the odd one out, Ananda decided he would attain enlightenment by the time of the meeting.

So he meditated with great determination for many hours each day.

On the last night before the Council, he still hadn't achieved enlightenment and there were only a few hours before the meeting would begin.

At this point Ananda decided to give up and get a couple of hours' sleep. He lay down on his bed.

It was then, before his head hit the pillow, that enlightenment dawned upon him.

The path of happiness

Whatever your Great Work is, I encourage you to do it.

Don't be afraid of the discomfort or pain you may encounter. Pain and pleasure are both part of life and part of Taking Action. You can only truly advance if you learn to deal with both.

When you do, you will see that your Great Work is the path of the most supreme satisfaction.

Take Action

Pursuing your Great Work is a path of happiness.

It is not a path *to* happiness but a path *of* happiness: happiness doesn't come from the outcome but from the path itself.

This is the reason you don't have anything to lose. Paradoxically, despite all the difficulties that I have warned you about in this book, winning is far easier than it seems.

As long as you are walking the path of your Great Work you are already making the world a better place and becoming a healthier, stronger, more authentic person.

Whether you attain the outcome you imagined at the outset is really less important than the person you become from pursuing it.

The bottom line is that you have every reason to Take Action in whatever way you can. The time to start is right now.

Printed in Great Britain
by Amazon

57816155R00116